Take It
To The MAX
The Ultimate Strategy
For Maximizing Profits and Growth
Jeff Peden, MEd.

Great Ideas Publications
Louisville

FIRST EDITION

ISBN 978-0-983129-1-5 (HC)

Take It To The MAX is available at special quantity
discounts to use as premiums, or for use in corporate
training programs. For more information, please send
inquiries to jeff@JEFFPEDEN.COM.

This book is dedicated to my wife
and best friend, Nancy,
whose love, support, and faith in me
carried me through the times
when I struggled;

and

to Bill Asher, who got me into all of this
in the first place.

CONTENTS

ACKNOWLEDGEMENTS

Thanks to Craig Kitch and Mike Coleman from the Tennessee Chapter of the National Speakers Association for prodding me; my editor Shanda Forish, who taught me how to write; Bernie Mudd, of Mudd Graphic Design Resources, LLC, who masterfully guided me through the manuscript layout; InSub Beckley and Eric Medley for their graphic arts expertise; my National Speaker Association colleagues Bob Wade, Anne Murray, Joe Bonura (who gave me the title for this book!), Stephen Tweed, Steve Rizzo, Greg Maciolek, Sandy Griffin, Marilee Driscoll, Larry Baltz, Greg Bennick and Mark LeBlanc; client support and encouragement from Randi Ballard, Courtney Crouch, Gary Owen, Bo Keltner, Lynette Owens, and Barrett Nichols; my Mastermind Group of Glenn Wilson, Steve and Rebecca Hoffman, Jennifer Hulse, Devin Best, and Vincent Berkun; my old classmate David McClure for legal advice; Stan and Donna Rosenthal, who so graciously include me on their weekly radio show; Dean Durling, Mike Murphy, Bob Graczyk, and John Shaninger at Quick Chek in Newark, NJ; and Melinda Simpson, Dick Wilson, Don Daub, Clem Wyman, Wayne Barber, John Bentley, Jeff Harper, Ted Rowan, Gary Rawlings, Angie Woodward, Bob Quaife, Hank Davis, Bill Ellis, Dean Hohl, Ernie Kilman, Jeff Burroughs, Darrin McCauley, Rick Schardein, Doug Helm, Rick Urschel, Mike White, Laura Wilson, Sheila O'Mara, Neil Atcher, Carole Jean Rogers, Gene Sprowl, and Jan Van Zant, without whose support this never would have happened.

Special recognition and thanks to John Britt, Partner at Mountjoy, Chilton, & Medley, CPAs, for his assistance in developing the implementation process for the ideas and strategies in the book; Sam Young, who artfully guided me through the development of graphics and promotional materials; and Al Cornish, CLO at Norton Health Care, who kicked ideas around with me and added clarity and direction. I'm very fortunate that they are good friends as well.

A special thank you to the countless number of people that I talked with while formulating the ideas in this book and who contributed their own ideas and insights to the project.

Finally, to my parents, Joe and Mary Peden, who could left me at a rest stop when I was young for all the excitement I caused. I am deeply grateful for your patience, forbearance and love.

INTRODUCTION

When I first began speaking on these ideas several years ago, I often wondered, "Aren't these ideas obvious to everyone? Am I just a blithering idiot repeating things people already know?" And then I looked around at the way most businesses in the United States were being run, and I realized that, if leaders *were* aware of these ideas, then very, very few were putting them to use.

From over 30 years in the business world, my personal experience affirms that the ideas in this book will help businesses maximize their potential. It works because it's based on the Biggest Ideas out there for your business, your customers, your people, and yourself. It's truly a win-win-win because it includes what's best for everybody.

The ideas in this book are easy to understand and inexpensive to implement. They are so simple that they're profound. Yet they are some of the most powerful ideas any organization can use to maximize their current potential, and position them to take full advantage of tomorrow.

This is not rocket science. I deliberately kept the content as brief as possible and the ideas as simple as possible so that you would have the easiest path to putting them into practice in your own organization.

If you're not having fun at work, if you're not excited about leaping out of bed in the morning and tackling the challenges the new day will bring, if your team isn't solidly behind you, giving you everything they've got, then you're not running your business from a high enough mountain top. You're down in the valley, thrashing around in the trees, when as a leader you should be looking out from a much broader field of vision to understand exactly what you should be doing to win the battle.

This book has two main goals. One is to describe an approach to running your business that delivers legitimate, sustainable growth and long-term profits. The other is to provide the framework for creating a workplace full of enthusiasm and energy, where every person feels like they're a part of something exciting, something special, something that means a whole lot more than going through the motions to make some money at the end of the day. A workplace where you'll attract and retain the best and the brightest because they want to be a part of what you've got.

This information works best for leaders who:

- *Get it.* They understand the value of the ideas and the powerful advantage of putting them into practice.

- They want to take action NOW, or at least decide on a firm start date.

- They want their culture built on positive values, and are committed to doing the right thing for their employees and their customers.

- They have a passionate desire to consistently deliver an Exceptional Customer Experience.

- They are optimistic and forward-thinking.

- They want work to be a fun and exciting place for their employees, who are focused on doing good things for their customers.

- They want to stay way ahead of their competition and maximize their profits.

This book is for organizations that want:

- **More** revenue, profits, repeat business, referrals, productivity, cooperation and teamwork; higher customer satisfaction and employee morale.

- **Less** employee turnover, workplace stress, indecision, bad attitudes, and workplace dysfunction.

Stay away from this book if you:

- Can't let go of autocratic leadership

- Think your employees are stupid and can't be trusted

- Want to come up with all the ideas and decisions by yourself

- Want to manipulate the customer into doing what you want, not what they want

The individuals and companies that are putting these ideas into practice are the most successful in the marketplace. In their pursuit of excellence, they rely on and benefit from the inclusion of other people and their ideas on how to create optimal success. You will find one such company described in Appendix A.

Finally, this book is about renewing hope. It's about elevating work to a higher level, to a level it was meant to exist at—the meaning and fulfillment work was meant to provide. Work can be fun, fulfilling, exciting—demanding the very best of us in exchange for creating outcomes we are proud of.

I hope you'll join the revolution.

There is only one good, knowledge,
and one evil, ignorance.
— SOCRATES

COMMON SENSE FOR BUSINESS

Once upon a time, a husband and his wife owned a goose named Lucky that laid a golden egg every day. They'd wake up in the morning, have a cup of coffee, go out in the back yard, pick up the goose, and take the golden egg to the bank. The wife loved the goose, and did her best to make sure it was comfortable and well-fed, but the husband couldn't have cared less about Lucky. He was impatient. He wanted to have it all *now*.

One night they were sitting around the kitchen table, having a glass of wine while discussing their 401k balances and retirement plans. The husband wanted to get rich faster, so they could retire *sooner* and move to the tropical isles. He was suspicious that the goose was holding out on them, that in fact, the goose was solid gold inside. He thought they could squeeze more money out of the goose *now*.

So, early the next morning, the husband snuck out of the house and choked the goose to death. But when he opened up the bird, he found that Lucky was just like every other goose. He realized *too late* that he had strangled the very source of their growing wealth and happiness.

When the wife found out what he had done, she strangled *him*, took their combined retirement savings, and moved to the tropical isles to live happily ever after, albeit with a bittersweet regret for poor *Lucky*.

There is a wide-spread epidemic among businesses in America. The name of the infection is GET RICH QUICK, no matter how it affects the customer or the long-term health of the organization. Many businesses, both great and small, are operating with policies and practices that are killing off the geese, their customers, who could be laying golden eggs for them every day. In an effort to have it all now, they're destroying their chances to have everything they want in the long run. They've forgotten that their customers are the very source of everything they want from their business. And they often overlook the welfare of their employees, the very people whose help they need to be successful.

What's at Stake?

Each business contains many sizable investments; consider them for a moment. Some are obvious and show up on the balance sheet, financed by entries on the income statement. They include:

- Premises (leased or owned)
- Equipment
- Capital Improvements
- Information Management Systems
- Marketing

- Business Development

- Cost of Goods Sold

- Operating Expenses

- Interest Expense

- Salaries and Wages

- Employee Benefits

- Owner Equity

What is the purpose of all this financial investment, or should we say, *risk*? It is to facilitate your business' health and success. But what about the costs that don't show up on the balance sheet when you play the GET RICH QUICK game? They are:

Lost customers: These are customers that were once yours but are now doing business with somebody else.

Lost referrals: These are referrals you no longer receive from the lost customers who don't like you anymore. In addition, some of them are warning everyone they know NOT to do business with you. On average, each lost customer tells up to 100 people, while a happy customer tells three.

Unhappy customers: These are customers that are not happy with you, but haven't found your replacement yet. In a world of nearly unlimited options, they soon will.

Lost great employees/leaders: These are people that used to work for you, and contributed to the success of your organization, but now work for someone else because they were not appreciated, short-changed by office politics, taken advantage of, expected to work in a toxic environment, didn't approve of what the company was doing to the customers (internal or external), or just got fed up with all the crap.

Unhappy employees/leaders: These are people that currently work for you and are frustrated, discouraged, marginally using their talents, or looking for a way out.

In an effort to reverse the damage caused by those factors, most businesses turn to advertising. It's amazing how much money is spent to get a new customer in the door, only for the customer to find that the product or level of service isn't even *close* to the expectation set by the advertising. Or, for the customer to be invited into a business only to find employees who couldn't care less about them, or worse, are waiting to exploit them. The customer doesn't miss the incongruity.

Advertising. Do you know what it really is? It's an invitation to come into your living room and check out who you are and what you offer. It's a blind date with a prospect. What preparations have you made to guarantee a WOW impression? When you invite someone to your home, don't you go out of your way to provide them the best experience possible?

Regrettably, the sequence of events typically goes something like this: You take hard-earned money out of your pocket and invest in advertising. You cross your fingers, and hope someone responds. They show up, and expect you to provide what the advertising promised.

What happens? What preparations have you made in advance to guarantee they have an incredible experience when they arrive? Do they have a can't-wait-to-come-back experience with you?

What's equally amazing is how companies treat their customers after the sale. For example, a customer has a problem and contacts the company. Sometimes the customer gets lost in voicemail purgatory. Sometimes the company won't return the phone call. Sometimes the company drags their feet, or refuses to make it right. As a result, the company loses twice. The company has spent money (now *lost money*) to add a new customer, and then furnished them with such a negative experience that the new customer is now a *lost customer* and a sworn enemy. The company would have been better off waiting to add customers until after they were prepared to deliver an exceptional customer experience. Unfortunately, all they accomplished was to spend their money creating another lost customer.

What is at stake is the health and welfare of your business. Both internal, with your employees, and external, with current and potential customers. The big question, therefore, is how to make both segments successful and lead your business on to great things.

LET'S BEGIN AT THE BEGINNING

What are we after in business? We're after higher sales, lower costs, and more profits—basic Business 101. What drives higher sales, lower costs, and more profits? *Customer growth, repeat business and referrals*, and *continuous improvements*. A business needs to create the strategies and procedures that reliably deliver an Exceptional Customer Experience, and then continuously work to make their business better and better as time goes on.

How do you consistently produce customer growth, repeat business, and word-of-mouth referrals? By becoming a *customer magnet*. You want to hang on to the customers you already have and attract as many new customers as possible. A lot of people know that it costs seven times as much to acquire a new customer than it does to keep an existing customer. So, why is it that so many businesses today have such a difficult time hanging on to the customers they already have? *It's because they're focused on the wrong thing.*

When I was a little boy, I used to hear men talking in the country store. One man would say, "I'm a Chevy man. All I'll ever buy is a Chevy." Another man would reply, "Well, I'm a Ford man myself. All I'll ever buy is a Ford. You couldn't give me a Chevy."

You know what I hear today? "I'm a Honda man. All I'll ever buy is a Honda." And someone will reply, "Well, I'm a Toyota guy myself. Hondas are all right, but I won't buy anything that doesn't have Toyota on it".

What happened? Poor management happened.

For the last 30 years, the Japanese have focused on making automobiles that are durable and dependable while improving product quality every year. Their focus has been on the *customer* and long-term company growth.

During the same period, the American Automobile Industry focused on making impressive-looking products with fancy options, but neglected to invest in research and development that would improve durability, reliability, and fuel economy. They focused on what would drive short-term *profits* rather than on what would drive long-term customer satisfaction and loyalty.

The Americans were focused on the wrong thing.

What's the cost of being focused on the wrong thing? When you don't deliver what the customer wants, you lose them to the competition. And when you operate your business at that level, you won't earn referrals. At that level, you're not a customer magnet. If you're not focused on delivering an Exceptional Customer Experience that generates customer excitement, you're not going to get *any* referrals or retain customers for long. It's like trying to fill a bucket that's got a hole in the bottom. You can keep pouring in new customers, but you've got to have something that grabs them or they'll pass right on through.

Too many in business today are focused on profits instead of a bigger purpose that attracts more customers. This misdirected focus on profits limits your return on investment. Profit is what you're after, but it's not the most important thing you're after. Profit is simply a way to measure how well you're playing the game. Focusing on profit as your *primary* strategy won't earn you the *most* money. Strange, isn't it? In order to maximize your profit, you must expand your horizon to include the best interests of the other people in the game, those that ultimately decide your fate.

To begin with, the return on investment that you need to worry about is your *customer's* return on *their* investment. The mistake has been to focus on stockholder's return on investment. The stockholder plays the game by making an educated guess as to what the customer wants, and antes up their investment in order to get a return. That's the risk they take. That's the game of business.

On the other hand, the customer's investment is ultimately the only one that matters. The customer is really in control of the game. If the customer doesn't invest in your company by buying what you offer, then the game for the stockholder is over. *Period.* Your primary focus must be on how you can maximize the *customer's investment.*

How do you maximize your customer's investment? By giving them better value than your competitors. This can be any combination of better service, respect, attention, dependability, honesty, value, delivery, or convenience. The list is limited only by your imagination. Do you want to be the market leader in your category or industry? Then take your focus off what's in *your* best interest and put it on giving the customer a greater return on *their* investment.

What are you focused on in *your* business? If you're doing things to manipulate short-term profits without considering the impact those actions have on your customers and employees, your *sales* aren't as high as they could be, your *costs* are much higher than they should be, and you leave a lot of *profits* behind.

What's the great idea behind all this? *Focus on the best interest of your customer and you'll get both profits and growth.*

We need to understand that if we are to successfully compete in the global economy, not to mention in our own domestic markets, we must do a better job delivering what the *customer* wants and putting their best interest as the top priority we focus on *every single day.* It's too easy today to lose a customer to a competitor if they're not happy with what you're giving them.

WHAT ARE THE DANGERS OF OUR PREOCCUPATION WITH PROFITS?

When we make profit the primary purpose of our company's existence, our *god*, we are tempted to excuse all sorts of behaviors that we would not tolerate in our personal relationships. We salve our conscience by telling ourselves, "It's just business." We tell ourselves that the end justifies the means. But is that really true?

It's as if we've convinced ourselves that the only way to be successful is to do whatever it takes to achieve our goals whether it causes problems for someone else or not. Is that really the limit of how big we can think?

And what is the reaction from our customers and employees to that approach?

- Loss of loyalty

- Suspicion

- Resentment

- Mistrust

- A desire to get even

Are these the outcomes you really want to create for your organization? How can you become a customer magnet if the way you run your business turns your customers and employees against you?

We can move our business to the next level of success only if we make serving our customers a higher priority than making money. If we make sure that what we offer serves their needs and delivers a consistent level of quality and value, along with an Exceptional Customer Experience, we won't have to worry about making money. Profits will follow automatically, and in great abundance!!

Have you ever had a customer experience with Nordstrom or Lands' End? They will do anything within their power to ensure your complete satisfaction. They will honor competitor's offers and take back returned merchandise without a question. Their employees are empowered to make your experience as pleasant and enjoyable as possible. I guarantee they hedge their bets on the belief that if they create an overwhelmingly favorable customer experience, you'll go back and tell your friends how wonderful they are. (I just did!)

It's crucial to understand that the way we make choices is based on what we think will maximize our payoff. Our only limitation is the breadth of our perspective, our awareness of all of the options we think might maximize the desired outcome. Take the following example.

There's a man who's been dreaming of a fishing boat. He's

already been to the boat show and picked out exactly what he wants. He knows it's going to cost him around $20,000. His dream is so big that he keeps it to himself.

He starts saving money. He takes baloney sandwiches to work instead of going out for lunch. On the weekends, he grills chicken for the family instead of steak. When they go on vacation, he encourages his family to stay in "efficiencies," so they can fix some of their own meals. He puts off buying the new suit he saw the last time he went to the mall. And after seven years, he finally has the money for the boat—*20,000 smackeroos*. He's so excited he's about ready to jump out of his skin.

Just as he's putting the last of his money in the bank, his daughter is graduating from high school. She's a class act who's studied hard and made very good grades. She wants to pursue a career in biochemistry and go to the one school her research indicates will give her the best education. *A very expensive school.* She's worked part-time jobs and saved what she could. She's received every scholarship that was available to her, but she's still a little short.

So she goes to her dad and says, "Dad, I need your advice. You know I want a career in biochemistry, and I've got the perfect school picked out. I've received every scholarship I qualified for, and I've saved the money I earned from my part-time jobs, but I'm still about $20,000 short. I know you don't have it, but can you think of any way I can come up with the rest of the money?"

The father loves his daughter very much. What does he do?

You might think that Dad, even though he must postpone his dream, would agree to give the boat money to help his daughter because he was being *unselfish*. But let's look at the ultimate consequences. If Dad kept the money and bought the boat, every time he went fishing he would think about his daughter losing out on the education she had worked so hard for, and he would feel *bad* about it. As a matter of fact, after a while, he wouldn't be able to look at himself in the mirror. On the other hand, if he gives the $20,000 to his daughter, he gets to feel good about himself that he was the kind of dad that would help his daughter fulfill her dreams.

What would *you* do?

The point is this: Every choice we make, whether or not it involves sacrifice, is determined by what we believe will give us the biggest payoff, the greatest reward. After reviewing all his options, the father made his choice based on the outcome he most wanted.

It's how we make decisions. Whether it's about our personal life or our business, we always strive to make the decision we think will give us the biggest payoff. The key to making the best choice is to calculate the ultimate value of every option and choose the one with the greatest reward. It's about how encompassing we can make our perspective.

If we use making a profit our primary intention for being in business, we're going to wind up making decisions that hurt our business in the long-run. This actually *impedes* us from maximizing our profits. If we could find a guiding light for our business that meets the needs of everyone in the game, we'd possess the right perspective to make better decisions. The truth is this: *Profits don't provide a big enough field of vision to maximize our return on investment.*

In order for you to achieve better results, you need to take your thinking to a higher level. If you don't take the time to clearly identify what strategy will lead you to the biggest payoff, you'll marginalize your return on investment. It's like saying: Ready, Fire, Aim. You'll probably hit something, but it might be the neighbor's cow instead of what you're really after.

So, how can you take your business to the max? If it's not in pursuing profits, what is it? There are three strategic priorities you must fully serve to maximize your Return on Investment. They are *your customers, your employees,* and *your company.*

Your first priority is your **Customers.** They want an exceptional experience, and to feel like you appreciate their business.

Your second priority is your **Employees.** They want to work for a company that provides them an opportunity for meaningful work, and to play an important role in its success. What leaders neglect to realize is just how important employees are in their company's success *or* failure. We recognize the value of our external customers, but our *internal* customers, our employees, are not recognized as a powerful secret weapon in the marketplace. Employees can make or break a company just as fast as external customers. Sometimes *faster.*

Your third priority is your **Company.** It experiences the hardiest growth by focusing on continuous improvement and delivering exceptional value, not only through what it offers, but by serving the wants and needs of its customers *and* employees.

These three priorities form a **Golden Triangle** that determines the success of your business. Cutting corners in serving any of the three priorities reduces your ROI.

When all priorities are fully served, you achieve three strategic outcomes:

- Company profits and growth

- Customer repeat business and referrals

- Employee engagement and productivity

This is the *path* to market leadership that puts you ahead and keeps you ahead of the competition.

What are your business' two biggest assets? *Your customers and your employees.* Your largest investment is in acquiring and retaining your customers, and underwriting the activities of your employees. With customers, you have a variety of expenses every year, including marketing, business development, and service. With employees, you spend money on wages and benefits; beyond that, you invest in the offices, tools, supplies and equipment they need to effectively perform their jobs. The problem *and* the opportunity is that businesses do not fully utilize their two biggest assets. How can you involve these two assets to grow your business and your profits?

The formula for success is this: The only way you can get everything *you* want as a business leader is to give your employees and your customers everything *they* want.

The temptation for a business leader is to assume that they're doing everything they need to do by providing an employee a job. The employer expects the employee to behave in a respectful and courteous manner with the customer. But it's sheer nonsense to expect your employees to treat your customers well if they work in an environment that doesn't treat them very well. A business is like a family. When you expect your child at home to behave a certain way, but they observe you exhibiting a *contradictory* behavior, the child gets a mixed signal and usually does whatever they see *you* doing. It's exactly the same at work. If your behavior towards your employees doesn't match the behavior you want to see from them, what can you honestly expect?

As leaders you must construct a united house wherein all occupants live by the same rules and expectations. *Leaders must set the example they want others to follow.* Leaders must abide by the same values and behaviors they expect their employees to provide for their customers. Then, employees will follow their lead and execute the behaviors that will create an Exceptional Experience for the Customer.

A *house divided against itself cannot stand.*
— ABRAHAM LINCOLN

Employees are often the most under-utilized asset a company has in its arsenal. Too many leaders view the employee as nothing more than someone that's being paid to do a job. What they don't realize is that employees have a wealth of knowledge and experience inside their heads: reservoirs of experience, wisdom, and creative solutions.

Your employees spend time with your customers every day. They hear what they have to say about what they like, what they don't like, and their suggestions for improvements. If leadership doesn't find out what their Employees know, they fail to acquire incredibly valuable information. This information would help leaders and managers make better decisions, solve problems, increase Employee morale, contribute to improving the Customer Experience, and reduce costs—the list goes on and on.

The Customer is the pivotal priority. This is where the potential for true growth resides. And yet so many times we're tempted to divert our attention away from doing what's best for the Customer because we're obsessed with tweaking earnings just a little bit *today*. As a result, we neglect doing what's best for the Customer and cripple our success. Is that a smart business strategy?

It costs seven times as much to acquire a new Customer as it does to keep an existing Customer. So, why not spend more of your time and resources on customer *retention*—on policies, procedures and initiatives—that help you hang onto your Customers?

The only reason a company exists
is to serve the Customer.
— PETER DRUCKER

Why are you spending such huge amounts of time and money on new customer acquisition when you're having such a difficult time keeping your existing customers from walking out the back door? You're underestimating the value of your existing Customers. You must continue providing them with what they expect every single day, in every single encounter, or you will disappoint them and lose out on their repeat business and referrals.

When you maximize all three priorities, you get:

Profits and growth. When you reconfigure the way you run your business in order to more effectively utilize the resources of your Employees and your Customers, you'll get a flow of information from your two biggest assets regarding what you can do to make your Company more successful, more attractive, more meaningful, and more durable. Profits and growth will inevitably follow (This isn't rocket science).

Improved Morale and Productivity. When you engage your Employees and include them on your team instead of treating them as a separate entity (i.e. management versus employees), you get an employee that's engaged, whose attitude improves, and whose productivity goes up.

Referrals. When you make your Customers your business *partners* by looking out for their best interest, they will respond with repeat business and referrals, and that is the *only* thing that creates true business growth.

So, the $1,000,000 question is: **How do we do that?**

THE EMPLOYEE PRIORITY

In 1847, a man in California heard the news that gold had been discovered in the southern part of the territory. His desire for gold was so great that he immediately sold his ranch and left for the riches he was sure to find.

The man who acquired the property was Colonel Sutter, and he built a mill on the stream that ran through the ranch. One day, the Colonel's daughter brought some sand from the millstream into the house to play with in front of the fire. As she sifted the sand through her fingers, the Colonel noticed something sparkling as the sand fell. The sparkling stuff was gold, and before long $38,000,000 worth had been excavated.

The man who sold out to Colonel Sutter wanted gold more than anything. He didn't realize what he wanted was *already* on his ranch. Had he known where to look, he could have had everything he wanted. Instead, he missed the opportunity that was right in front of him.

Are you overlooking the obvious in your own organization? Are there vast amounts of gold right in front of you? There is if you know where to look for it. It is in the form of a wealth of ideas, insights, and initiative buried inside your *employees*. They are the most overlooked asset your organization possesses that it can use to leverage its potential and achieve its goals.

A lot of companies attempt to maximize profits without enlisting the help of one of their biggest assets. However, in order for a Company to maximize its Return on Investment, the first step towards success is to do something counterintuitive. The first step a Company needs to take is to create a unified TEAM with their employees because *they* are the ones the Company depends upon to deliver an Exceptional Experience for their Customers, and they have lots of great ideas on how to do that.

A company cannot deliver a consistent Exceptional Customer Experience that generates referrals and repeat business without the full support and cooperation of their employees.

When your employee interacts with your customer, your employee *is* your company to that customer. Your employee is the only person in your company the customer knows. *It's critical to understand how much your success depends on your Employees.* There are no unimportant team members. Everyone in your organization touches the customer in some way and plays an essential role in the Customer Experience.

Let's take a moment and look at some of the different ways organizations are structured. Almost every organization has all the pieces of the puzzle they need to be successful.

Some organizations have pieces of the puzzle that know what job they're specifically assigned to do, and

A company is the people that work there.
— MICHAEL DUKE

even what department they report to, but they don't understand how they're connected with the other parts. As a result, the individual pieces achieve a certain level of output, but don't understand how to work together to achieve the *biggest* output.

When the parts of your organization don't understand how they depend on each other to maximize results, then everyone is *on their own* to make it work. No one in Leadership has ever explained the Big Picture, so the employees don't understand how to work together in the best way. They don't see that if everyone worked together they would achieve better results. This type of organization usually struggles to survive.

In other organizations, some pieces of the puzzle are connected together as *departments,* but don't understand how they connect to the rest of the company. Departments achieve a certain level of effectiveness within their own group, but don't see how they depend on the other departments to maximize their own success. This lack of understanding gives birth to *silos.* When you have silos, the separate departments resent each other and resist cooperation. They don't have a big enough frame of reference to grasp how much they truly need each other. This causes silos to either work against each other, creating *turf wars,* or in different directions, causing *chaos.* This short-sightedness not only threatens the Customer Experience, but undermines the effectiveness of the entire organization.

Finally, some companies have leaders who understand that in order to create the best results, all the pieces of the puzzle must be connected properly and work together. They have a clear picture of who they are, how they are interdependent, and where they are going. The purpose of the organization is understood by all. The potential for the sum to become greater than the individual parts is realized. Everyone works together because they know *why* their job is important, what part it plays in the success of the organization, and how everyone else depends on them to do *their* job successfully. When an organization works together in harmony, they outperform their competition and achieve significantly higher levels of growth and profits.

MATCHING VALUES

Let's look at the concept of motivation. You cannot motivate your employees unless you first tap into what has meaning for them and triggers their passion. You must find a way to motivate them *internally*. You must first understand what's important to them in *their* life— their values. If you're not leading your team with a set of values that complements theirs, you can try to motivate them externally all day long, but it won't do any good.

If you ask employees to do something that conflicts with their personal values, they're going to resist. Resistance can show up in many ways other than outright revolt. It can be observed as a loss of enthusiasm, loss of productivity, negative attitudes, or passive/aggressive behavior.

In addition, if an organization expects their employees to take actions that could have a negative effect on the customer, many employees will either look for a way around it or find a way to avoid it, if at all possible. Many employees want no part of delivering shoddy products or services, deliberate misrepresentation, or a lack of follow through on what was promised to the customer. Organizational pressure to violate personal standards prevents many Employees from putting their heart into their work.

If you want your employees to support your goals, you must create a work environment that reflects *positive* values that they can rally around. Let's be honest. As a leader, do you want a work environment that tolerates employees you can't trust? Do you want people working for you that only care about what's in it for them, but don't consider what's best for you and the Company? Do you want employees working for you that you can't depend on, or that are dishonest with you? Of course not.

So, doesn't it make sense to promote and support a culture at work that models the same values, attitudes, and behaviors you want from your employees? For that matter, what attitudes and behaviors will get the most positive response from your customers? Wouldn't it make sense that in order to ask for and receive the best from your employees, your *leaders* must first promote a cultural mindset within your own Company that focuses on doing what's best for your customers *and* employees?

The most effective strategy to earn the respect, loyalty and trust of your Employees is to set high ethical standards and non-negotiable expectations of excellence throughout your entire organization. One powerful standard is doing what's best for the Customer. *A corporate culture that's focused on doing what's best for the Customer creates the psychological and emotional incentive for your Employees to do what's best for the Company.* This establishes a solid foundation your company can build long-term success upon. This brand of leadership inspires the best from your employees and forges the highest levels of commitment to excellence.

How can you create optimum outcomes any other way? You must provide your employees with a work environment that replicates the behaviors and attitudes you expect of them. Otherwise, you create an obvious contradiction that no one will believe in or follow. When leadership has the courage and commitment to model the attitudes and behaviors they want to see in their employees, then employees will put their enthusiasm and efforts behind doing their best for you and the organization. As a result, your TEAM is empowered to consistently deliver an exceptional experience for your customers.

WHY DO YOU HAVE MORALE AND PRODUCTIVITY ISSUES WITH YOUR EMPLOYEES?

I heard a statistic a few years ago that 75% of Americans hate their jobs. When somebody hates their job, they typically do only enough to get by. They don't want to get fired because they have to pay their bills, so they do just enough to hang on. They give far less than 100%.

Your employees want a place to earn a living where work means more than a paycheck. They dread going in to work when the only thing that's motivating them is money. They have no stake in the game other than holding on to their job.

Without purpose or meaning, each day becomes an exercise in survival. The goal becomes getting to the end of the day, and the end of the week. "Hump Day" and "Livin' for the weekend" reflect the lack of meaning their work provides, rather than seeing work from the bigger perspective of offering an opportunity to express talents and realize dreams.

Many employees do not understand the real meaning of *why* they do their job. No one in leadership has ever explained the *purpose* of their work. Employees are left on their own to define the meaning of what they do every day. In the absence of a clear purpose, they often view work as nothing more than a way to pay their bills. When work is reduced to that level, there's not a whole lot left to get excited about.

How can you create meaning for the work everyone does in your organization? The answer lies in creating a big enough *why*—the *purpose* of your organization—*why* it delivers *what* it delivers to your Customers. Is the purpose of your organization to make your Customers better off than before they met you? Is it to help your Customers solve their problems or add value to their lives? Have you created a big enough *why* for your organization for your employees to really care?

Have you ever been involved in a volunteer effort? Something you felt made a real difference in the world? You can easily come up with a list of reasons *not* to volunteer. You have to give up your free time. You don't get paid for doing it. As a matter of fact, it usually costs money out of your own pocket in one way or another. Sometimes, you don't even get to see the end result of your efforts. So, why do you do it?

You volunteer because the purpose behind your efforts *means* something to you. You want to be involved in doing something worthwhile because you want to make a difference with your life. When you can make a difference with your life, you feel good about yourself. Many of your employees want to get the same feeling from their work. They want to be part of something that makes a positive impact on the world around them. If leadership could articulate to everyone that the purpose of the company was to make a positive difference in the lives of their customers, define exactly how they accomplished that, and backed that up with congruent actions towards both employees and customers, wouldn't employees connect with that deeper meaning of work and put their hearts back into their efforts?

If you can redefine the purpose of work as the way your organization makes its own positive difference in the lives of others, you'll create better outcomes. You'll get stronger employee buy-in and engagement, higher levels of customer satisfaction, and you'll generate enthusiasm, enjoyment, and the mechanism for personal fulfillment.

If that statistic about 75% of Americans hating their jobs holds true in your organization, there's a pretty good chance that three-quarters of the people working for you don't really want to be there. If you have a substantial number of Employees that are working at 50 or 60% of their potential, can you afford the weight of that handicap? Do you have any idea what that costs your organization?

Let's do a little back-of-the-envelope math. Grab a calculator and:

• Write down your annual payroll

• Add the cost of benefits (health insurance, 401K contributions, vacation/sick days, etc)

- Multiply the result by 50% (conservative estimate of the percentage of your employees not fully engaged)

- Multiply the remaining number by 25% (gap between employee potential and current level of effort)

This provides a rough estimate of the annual cost to your organization for not fully engaging your employees. Isn't that a big enough number to make you want to get these folks on board 100%? Wouldn't it be *good business* to find a way to do that?

BEING INCLUDED

Another limiter to morale is that Employees don't feel included when decisions are being made. Research indicates that if you want someone to go along with the final decision, you must include them in the process. At the very least, ask them for their ideas and input, so that when a decision is made and change occurs, they don't feel completely left out. Human nature makes us want to be a part of whatever is going on.

I remember being on the playground at grade school during recess. We would pick a game to play and two people would choose sides. Sometimes the game had room for everybody and sometimes it didn't. I remember standing on the playground with my heart pounding, hoping that I would get chosen to be part

Those who help plan the battle
don't battle the plan.

of the game. One of the worst things we can experience is the feeling of being left out, like we're not good enough or important enough to be included. Your Employees feel left out when they're not included in decisions regarding matters that directly affect them.

One of your most valuable assets is what is locked away inside the minds of your employees. I've heard businesses over the years include in their advertising, "Our people are our greatest asset." The irony of that statement is that most business leaders rarely dig into the wealth of knowledge and experience of their own gold mine.

How often do you encourage your employees' input? Too often leadership assumes that they know what is going on in the marketplace, what's causing the problems and what are the best solutions. That's myopic and success-*limiting*. So many times, in working with clients, I have uncovered great ideas and creative solutions to problems that have plagued the organization for years coming from their very own employees who are directly involved with the problem itself.

For example, take an Employee working on an assembly line. They've done that job for years. They know the job inside and out. There's a good chance they've identified some problems and have ideas on how to solve them. They've noticed things that could reduce costs and save the Company money, improve worker safety, or increase Customer value. But nobody in leadership asks them for their ideas. Turning a deaf ear to valuable employee insights costs organizations vast amounts of profit every year.

Encourage your people to share ideas about what they notice that can improve your business. The people that work for you have an incredible amount of talent, imagination, and ideas that can help you take your organization to a higher level. It is leadership's *responsibility* to find out what they have to offer. When you include them as an integral part of your success, they'll get excited about their job, feel important, and help you be more successful. They'll be working *with* you instead of just earning a paycheck.

THE IMPORTANCE OF TEAM

Yet another reason for low morale and productivity is that Employees don't feel a connection with a *team*. Quite often, there is a team in theory, but not one in practice. Instead, ungoverned internal competition, politics, and personal favoritism discourage cooperation and marginalize results. Leaders must take the initiative and structure the work environment so that everyone knows what's expected and is treated equally. In order to create the biggest result, leaders must point out that everyone on the team is accountable and expected to support the success of everyone else.

Employees want to be part of a team that works together. That doesn't mean there is not a proper place for competition. Competition is useful in a number of ways. Competition drives creativity; it spurs us to come up with new solutions to problems and create new products and services. But inside the *family* of the organization, employees shift into a higher gear when there is a sense of camaraderie and shared purpose to their work. A work environment is far more effective and enjoyable when employees see themselves working *together* to compete against an opponent *outside* of the organization.

THE IMPACT OF ATTITUDES

When Employees feel overlooked and underappreciated, they can develop a "me" versus "them" mentality.   Their   behavior   becomes   antagonistic, uncooperative, and resentful. And it undermines the effectiveness of everyone it touches.

When employees feel the organization doesn't care about them, they develop negative attitudes. The effects of negative attitudes have been studied in organizations for years. Someone with a negative attitude influences many people and contributes to a negative attitude in others. Conversely, someone with a positive attitude in the workplace influences fellow workers in a positive way. Productivity goes up with positive attitudes; productivity goes down with negative attitudes. When your employees sense that you notice and appreciate what they do, it goes a long way towards fostering positive attitudes.

WHAT CAN ORGANIZATIONS DO TO GET THE BEST AND THE MOST FROM THEIR EMPLOYEES?

Here are some suggestions to engage, include and inspire your employees. These suggestions do not exhaust the possibilities. Rather, they are meant to serve as a jumpstart for your own creative juices, a launching pad to initiate the process and make it your own.

Ask for their ideas. Remember that untapped gold mine of ideas that is locked inside every one of your Employees' heads? Their input will help your business grow more effectively by solving problems, reducing costs, improving efficiencies, and working more effectively with customers. You'll never find out what they see, hear and know *unless you ask them.* Every Employee has a unique set of perspectives and insights because they are the ones performing a particular job. It's impossible for you to know what they know because *you're not doing their job.* You've got your hands full with your own job.

I've got a friend and client, Gary Owen, in Louisville, KY, who is number two in sales volume (out of 600 in the world) in the Allegra Print & Image franchise system. He has put this strategy into practice by involving his employees in discovering opportunities to save money and improve his printing business. Recently, in one pre-press meeting, one of his employees had determined that their printing capacity could be increased by 15-20% if they would use a slightly larger paper stock. Using the larger paper stock would eliminate a paper curling issue that had limited the speed of the press.

Another employee figured out how a change in print set-up would eliminate steps in the cutting and finishing process. He realized that they could reduce the number of cuts if they would just rearrange how the images were organized on the press sheet so that full bleeds would be back to back, reducing the number of cuts and therefore saving additional process time. Gary said these two ideas alone increased production by 30-35%, reduced overall costs by 7% in the bindery department, and added approximately 2% of profit to the bottom line. To say the least, Gary is very excited about the outcomes he has achieved so far by engaging his employees and leveraging their knowledge and experience!

When you ask for their ideas, you're killing two birds with one stone. First, you're giving your Employees one of the major things they want from their work. You're including them and demonstrating your respect of their value to your organization. You're telling them you rely on their input and advice to help the Company be as successful as it can possibly be, and, by doing so, you make them an important part of your team.

Second, you're getting valuable new ideas about how to improve the organization while subconsciously triggering increases in their productivity, teamwork, and cooperation. Attitudes are improving, turnover and absenteeism are going down, and fewer mistakes are being made because Employees are now finding meaning in their jobs and are taking greater pride in what they do. *And it doesn't cost you a dime.* As a matter of fact, you're achieving far better results while reducing your own stress level because *you don't have to come up with all the ideas by yourself anymore.* You've got a team behind you that's got your back and helping you succeed at *your* job.

Connect your team. As you move forward with the process of engaging your Employees, *have every level of management commit to a personal meeting with every single direct report on their team.* This must occur from the CEO's team all the way through to the front-line Employees. If you overlook anyone or any part of this process, you're communicating to your Employees they're really *not* important, just as they suspected.

Before each meeting, take the time to define the contribution that each one of your team members makes to the Company. Do your homework on the specifics of each Employee's involvement and how they impact the rest of the organization *and* the Customer. Identify at least two examples of how someone else in the organization depends on how well they execute their job responsibilities.

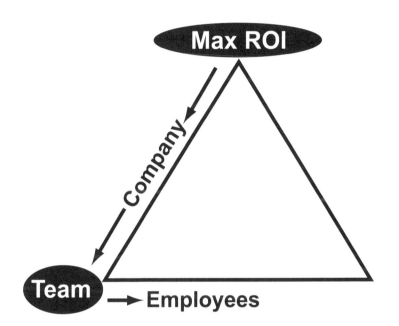

Then, take the time to sit down with each employee, cover each item on the agenda thoroughly, and discover their internal motivators. Do NOT have this meeting over e-mail or the telephone, no matter how busy you are. The long-term ramifications are far too great. The only way to create the end result you want is to genuinely connect with them in person. Your words *and* actions must communicate to every employee how valuable they are to your team and the organization.

Make the meeting important! Don't underestimate the emotional impact it will have on each employee or overlook the valuable outcomes that will occur as a result. If at all possible, take them away from the office. Take them out to lunch or at least out for a cup of coffee. Give this meeting the time and attention it requires to convey special significance. The objective is to emphasize how important *they* are and how much you depend on the role they play and the contributions they make. Every minute you genuinely invest in your team will give you multiple returns in their attitude, cooperation, and productivity.

When you sit down with them, communicate the following:

- How much you appreciate what they do

- How important their job is to the Company and how it impacts the other departments in the Company

- How much you and the other team members are counting on them

- How their specific job touches the Customer Experience

If you're not comfortable with sincerely communicating these critically important concepts to your direct reports, get out of leadership! People *won't* follow you if they don't think you truly care about them.

Here are some suggestions for the conversation. You will eventually want to put this into your own style and words. When you meet with your direct report, sit down with them and say something like this:

"First, I want to tell you how much I appreciate what you do for our organization. Your _____ job is an important part of what we do here. And I want you to know that our customer development and retention efforts would not be as successful if it were not for the contribution your work makes to our customers' experience. I want you to know how much everyone is depending on you, because they can't do their job successfully without you.

"I also want you to know that I need your input and suggestions so that I can do the very best job for you, the team, and the company. I want to hear every idea you have about how we can run this business better and better. Every day is an opportunity for improvement. Please feel free to bring me any idea you have, regardless of how crazy it may seem to you. And, if you give me an idea we can use to make our business better, I want to say "thank you" in a way that means something special to you. Please tell me how I can show my appreciation for your ideas."

As you listen to their response, keep in the back of your mind that in order to motivate someone else, you must first tap into what means something for them. During the meeting, ask them about their personal goals, their most important values, and what rewards they'll work hard to achieve. You will then be able to align the goals you set for them with the payoff they want.

As the conversation progresses, ask them what they think about what the two of you are discussing and *write down what they say*. You'll want to include their specific thoughts and motivators in their personal file for future reference. Give them the opportunity to respond and open a line of communication with you. This is very important. *You're on the threshold of a powerful new partnership*. Both of you may be a little nervous, but the important thing is to get the conversation going. The sincerity of your actions will be far more important to them than the actual words you use. They're watching to see if you really mean what you're saying. You want this to be the first step towards a more effective and productive relationship with your team members.

Do your best to come away from the meeting with a clear understanding of how to reward them for their ideas and how to build upon your initial conversation at a future date. As far as individual motivators, one could be a gift certificate to a favorite restaurant, so they could celebrate their accomplishment at work with a spouse. For others, it might be a memo circulated throughout the workplace acknowledging their idea and how it was used. For still others, their reward could be a few hours off with pay so they can go to their 6th grader's Little League baseball game being played during working hours. Can you imagine the loyalty and enthusiasm you would infuse in your employees if you made their recognition personal through something that was important to them? They'd run through brick walls for you!

What do your employees really think of you? Do they think you work hard to support their success? That you care about them as real people? That you listen to their ideas? That they can trust you? If your answer is, "I don't know and I don't care. I'm paying them to do their job and they better do it or else," then you are on treacherous ground. If you don't know the answer to these questions, it would be smart to find out. Because if your employees don't think you care about them, you not only marginalize their attitudes and productivity, you run the risk of losing your best managers and employees to someone who *will* care and make them feel important. People today want to work for someone they trust to lead them with a positive and caring attitude about *everyone* on the team.

When you genuinely connect with your employees and they see the sincerity and commitment of your words by the consistency of your actions, you'll improve their buy-in about *your* ideas and the direction you want to lead them. You'll increase their productivity by honoring their values and giving them what *they* want and, as a result, get more of what *you* want.

Empower your team. You're the leader. *So lead.* People generally live up to the expectations you have about them. Don't be afraid to set your expectations high! They will respond enthusiastically to your confidence and trust in them.

What they see you do will be the example they will imitate. Set the rules of the game and clearly define the playing field. What are their boundaries? What can they be empowered to do within those boundaries? What can you delegate to them to manage themselves? Very few people enjoy being micro-managed. People want to be trusted with the responsibility to do their jobs competently without constant surveillance. Empowerment, along with a healthy dose of trust and encouragement, takes the lid off and lets the best a person has to give bubble to the top.

Give your team Clear Targets to aim at. Here's an example of a fairly typical Mission Statement:

We shall surpass customer's expectations through dedication to anticipating and satisfying customer needs while providing services of superior quality, value and delivery through teamwork.

What does that really mean? If you were an employee of this company, would you know what to do? Could you identify the target, know what specific actions to take, and absolutely know when you hit the goal?

As leaders, give your employees very specific, concrete targets that everyone can understand in order to make the right decisions and take the right actions to support the organization's success. They need a goal that's clear and simple enough so they can ask themselves, "Is what I'm about to do right now going to move us closer to our goal or farther away?" They need an easy-to-use map and compass to help them stay on track.

How many husbands get excited and drop whatever they're doing when they hear their wife say, "Honey, let's go shopping." Not many. But what if your wife says, "Honey, I want you to go shopping with me and help me find a pair of red shoes." Your ears perk up and you feel your nose give a little bloodhound sniff. A clear target begins to form in your mind. She says, "Honey, I want you to go shopping with me and help me find a pair of red shoes with black bows on the front." You feel your tail begin to wag and the hair on the back of your neck start to rise. Then, she says, "Honey, I want you to help me find a pair of red shoes with a black bow on the front and two-inch heels." Now you're running around the living room, barking and pawing at the door. You have been given a very specific target. You know what to go after while you're in the shoe store (and what will get you back home!).

In the same way, when you give your team a clear and well-defined goal, they will know what they are going after and whether they are hitting the bull's eye or not.

Let's summarize: In order for a Company to maximize its ROI, the first step is to create a TEAM with the Employees—a team in which the Leaders work with each and every Employee to help them understand that they're appreciated, the importance of their job, how everyone else on the team is depending on them, and what their personal connection is with the Customer Experience. You've taken the time to meet with them one-on-one and open up a dialog about what makes them tick and what will personally reward them for outstanding contributions. Building upon this, you develop a relationship with your direct reports that deepen mutual trust, respect, and cooperation.

Walls between Leaders and Employees must be torn down. There are not different levels of importance regarding team members, only different responsibilities to be executed. Silos and other dysfunctional barriers that interfere with communication, cooperation, teamwork and optimal outcomes must be abolished.

As leaders, you must engage and include your Employees so they really *get it* that you want them on your team and are thoroughly involved in playing a vital role with everything. Then, when you've created this seamless team without barriers or silos, everyone knows they can depend on the encouragement and support of leadership to work with them to create an Exceptional Customer Experience.

Everyone on the TEAM, leaders *and* employees, finally have their eyes focused in the same direction. You're beginning to look out for each other. Trust and cooperation is building, and *work is starting to become fun and to mean something.*

THE CUSTOMER PRIORITY

December 24, 1983 was the coldest Christmas Eve on record. My wife and I were on our way south for a year-end vacation, but the weather was getting so bad that the airlines were struggling to keep their flights on schedule, and as the day wore on, it became obvious we weren't going to make our final connection. We were going to spend Christmas Eve in Atlanta, in the *airport*. Five of us were left stranded in the Delta terminal. After our flights had been rescheduled for early the next morning, we were ushered into a waiting room off the main terminal, the warmest spot in the area. We accepted our fate and made ourselves as comfortable as possible. Midnight was not far away.

A man stuck his head in the door and asked us what was going on. He was bundled up in about as much clothing as one person could wear, looking like the Michelin Man. After he heard our story, he told us to wait there. About 20 minutes later, he reappeared and announced that we were coming with him. We walked out of the terminal to a parking lot, and got into his station wagon. He explained that he was taking us to his house for the evening and would get us back to the airport in time to catch our flights the next morning.

In a short time, we were sitting in a warm house, eating freshly baked cookies, and watching a movie on

TV. It turned out that he was a baggage handler for Delta and was just getting off work when he heard that we got stuck overnight. He took it upon himself to do something for us since it was Christmas Eve.

At about four in the morning, we bundled back up and he drove us to the airport to catch our flights. I never saw the man again, and I don't remember his name. I wish I did. But I'll tell you this: the memory of that night still burns brightly in my mind, almost 27 years later. He gave us something that, in a way, was one of the best gifts I've ever received. That night, he reached inside of himself and gave us all a part of his *heart*.

For many years after, my first choice of airlines to fly was Delta.

It's all about the customer, isn't it? It's all about doing such a great job that our customers not only return to shop with us again and again, they refer us to people that like and trust them—their friends. But it's also about creating such a vivid, extraordinary experience for our customers that they never really consider doing business with anyone else. They don't need to because they've got us to take care of them.

In order to create a consistent Exceptional Customer Experience, the TEAM must filter every decision made and action taken regarding the customer through **One Rule**:

Always do what's in the best interest of the Customer.

Always do what's in the best interest of the Customer.

Every single time. Even if it costs you something in the short-run. Even if it means you recommend a competitor because you don't have the best solution for a particular Customer need. I can hear your heads exploding. "What!?! Are you crazy?!? I'm not going to recommend a competitor and lose a sale!" Let me tell you a secret I learned the hard way: If you don't look out for the best interest of your Customers, you're going to lose their business anyway.

You've had access to this secret for a long time. You've probably seen and heard it countless times, once or twice during every holiday season with friends and family. Most of us could say that we grew up with the answer. It was just too obvious. Get out your copy of *Miracle on 34th Street* (1947) and forward until the time counter says 26:51. For the next 67 seconds, you will hear Mr. Macy describe the secret to his senior leadership staff, and the rewards he was certain they would reap.

The *One Rule* is the ultimate strategy for maximizing profits and growth. This is *the* Strategic Play—the highest level of thinking for attracting and retaining customers for a lifetime. The One Rule must be the primary filter for every plan of action you take in your business.

Here's another way to understand The One Rule: Don't do anything to piss your customers off! You'll get yourself in trouble if you think it's more convenient for you to do business to satisfy *your* needs. I have worked for

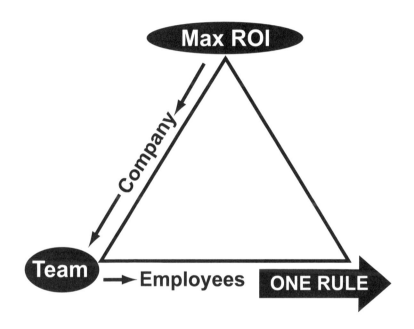

organizations that said, "The customer is just going to have to do business *our* way." That's absolutely the *worst* attitude you can have if your goal is to hang on to your customers! It's not about *you*, it's about *them*. If your customers don't think your way of doing business is convenient for *them*, they'll find someone else to give them what they want. *Bend over backwards* to make it easy for your customers to do business with you.

When I was in sales, I was terrified at the thought of selling something to someone that wasn't in their best interest. Because in the back of my mind, I remembered all the times someone sold me something that didn't fit my needs and I never wanted to do business with them again.

So, I worked really hard to make sure I asked all the right questions and got a solid feel for what they needed. Only then did I look inside my little black bag to see if what I had was going to help them meet their objective. Sometimes I didn't have it, so I recommended another company, along with names and phone numbers. And a funny thing happened. The people that had been referring me gave me even *more* referrals.

Coincidence? I don't think so. I had discovered a rule to follow that allowed my sales efforts to flourish, and for me to go home feeling good about how I was doing the right thing for others. Because of how I was serving the needs of my customers and safeguarding the reputation of my referral partners, I became an even bigger *custom-*

er magnet. They liked me. They trusted me. And they wanted to do business with me because everyone got what they wanted. Did the One Rule work? It helped me become the number one salesperson in the entire country.

Success comes when we help the customer win. When the customer wins, we get everything we want: growth, profits, and the personal satisfaction of adding value to the businesses and lives of other people, just like us.

Remember, if it weren't for your customers, you wouldn't have a business. Your customers are the ONLY reason you are in business. If you think that you're in the business for profit, and you forget the fact that you're in business *because* of your customers, then you open the door for bad things to happen. Businesses need to be brought back to ground zero: *it's all about the customer.*

What's the flip side of the Biggest Payoff? *The Biggest Loss.* The Biggest Loss happens when your customer finds out that you have not been looking out for their best interest. They then become a liability that tells the world all the reasons not to do business with you. No amount of marketing or advertising spin can fix that problem.

Following the One Rule is the most effective and reliable way to build customer trust and loyalty. The customer puts their faith in you to do what's best for them. To misuse that trust risks far more than the current sale. You risk the customer finding out their trust has been violated. When that happens, the Customer never buys from you again. *You lose all future sales.* Wouldn't it be a far better business decision to help your Customer get the right solution today and be regarded as their trusted advisor for all future purchases?

Success is a long-term game. True long-term business growth, consistent profits, and insulation from external threats (such as new competition or business recessions) come from following the One Rule. You breathe life into the kind of customer loyalty that puts you out in front of your competitors and generates referrals because they trust you enough to recommend you to their friends. If you don't follow the One Rule, you put everything at risk you've worked so hard to achieve. Are you that big of a gambler?

WHAT BUSINESS ARE YOU IN?

Whether you realize it or not, you're in the *referral business*. Every action you take should be aimed at creating the kind of experience with your customers that leads them to telling someone else how wonderful you are and that they should be doing business with you. It's the least expensive way to grow your business and the most effective way to add new customers immediately.

The thought that should be running through your mind when you work with customers is: *How can I*

*We fall in love with someone,
not from how we feel about them,
but how they make us feel
about ourselves.*

— ANNE MURRAY

earn your referral? Forget focusing on customer satisfaction. Customer satisfaction doesn't mean anything anymore. That keeps you from losing. Referrals get you ahead in the game. What you want to know from your customers is: "What kind of experience do I need to provide for you that you get so excited about, you want to tell your friends and neighbors about us?"

Everything you do, every interaction you have with your customers, creates a positive, neutral, or negative experience. They all result in what your customer will say about you.

A *positive* experience causes them to want to do business with you again, and spread the word about how wonderful you are.

A *neutral* experience is a ho-hum experience where their immediate needs were met, but you disappear from their minds as soon as they walk out your door, hang up the phone, or turn off their computer.

A *negative* experience causes them to avoid you in the future if at all possible, and talk bad about you when the opportunity arises.

Developing a relationship with a customer is a lot like dating. Whether or not they say yes to the next one depends on their experience of you during this one. Do you remember how you acted when you were dating someone? Your imagination searched for all the ways you could present yourself in the best light so they would fall madly in love with you. That's exactly the same strategy you want to use with every customer you have. You want to be their *Love Potion Number 9*. You want them to fall in love with you and think of no one else when it comes to what you offer. That is your ultimate goal—to grow your business by delivering a customer experience so exceptional that your competition fades into the distance.

In order for your customers to want to give you their business and their referrals, you must give them something they like so much that they *want* to refer you. If you or your employees are just "doing your job" you're probably not creating the kind of customer experience that makes them want to grab everyone they know and tell them what an incredible experience they had with you.

Have you heard of the Pareto Principle? It's the 80/20 rule. Eighty percent of your business comes from twenty percent of your customers. Eighty percent of your results come from twenty percent of your efforts. Your customers can also be divided into an 80% group and a 20% group. Twenty percent of your customers are *not* loyalty-driven. They typically care only about themselves and what they can extract from life. They want something for nothing. If you bring them on board as a customer, they will take up most of your time, be the most demanding, and leave as soon as they think they can get what they want cheaper from someone else. There is no loyalty, no reciprocation.

The good news is that eighty percent of your customers *are* loyalty-driven. They offer you the opportunity to build a relationship with them, and in return for exceptional service become repeat customers, and refer you to people they know.

People give you their business, and ultimately their loyalty and referrals, because they *know* you, they *like* you, and they *trust* you. It's called the know/like/trust factor. And it just happens to be the key ingredient of your ultimate success or failure. We know it's important, unless we're part of the 20% that only care about ourselves and prey on others.

Forget about the 20% that have no loyalty. If you get their business some of the time, consider it found money. The real opportunity for your business lies with the 80%. In fact, the 80% comprises such a vast number of possible customers that your business does not have the capacity to serve them all. Compared to your resources, their number is practically infinite but, be fairly warned, they are a group with high expectations.

How many of you realize that every Customer gives you a test when they do business with you? They have five questions about you, and based on the grade you receive, decide if they like you enough to come back. It's an emotional test. People make important decisions based on emotion and justify them intellectually afterwards.

The first question Customers have is: **Can I trust you?**

What is the most important thing in your world? What can realign your priorities in an instant? Your safety. When your safety is being threatened, nothing else matters. You will do anything to be safe again. And behind safety with others is a thing called trust. When you trust someone, you feel safe with that person. When you do business with someone that you trust, you will go along with what they suggest much faster than with someone that you just met.

People will spend their money with people they know, like, and trust because they feel safe with them. They know if something goes wrong, they can get the problem fixed without any hassles. It's easier and safer than doing business with a stranger.

Lack of trust causes big problems in the business world and makes everything more expensive. New business takes longer to develop, contracts take longer to sign, and customers are slower to give us their loyalty. But isn't the general lack of trust about business a huge opportunity for you? What if you took advantage of that and ran your business so that it generated confidence and appreciation from your customers rather than frustration and resentment?

Trust is the key question everybody has about you. Trust is the cornerstone you can build upon to become the market leader and customer favorite. If your customers don't trust you, they will base their buying decisions solely on price. *How many of you want to compete solely on price?*

The second question is: **Do you care about me?**

I read a story of how State Farm Insurance handled homeowner claims after the devastation of Hurricane Andrew. While the other insurance companies refused to renew policies, State Farm did a very unusual thing: they not only renewed their customers' policies, they investigated the cause of why so many roofs were damaged during the storm. They found that the roofs were not anchored properly, so in addition to paying the claims, they gave their policy holders additional funds to properly anchor their roofs. The other insurance companies shook their heads in disbelief. Why would State Farm do that?

State Farm was doing something intuitively brilliant. Not only did they strengthen their relationship with customers, they reduced their exposure to future claims. Who do you think is now the insurance company of choice with homeowners in South Florida?

Looking out for ourselves is easy. But what could you gain if you raised your level of thinking up to the bigger idea of looking out for the best interest of others as much as your own? Like State Farm, our position is always strength-

We cannot tell the precise moment when friendship is formed. As in filling a vessel drop by drop, there is at last a drop which makes it run over; so in a series of kindnesses there is at last one which makes the heart run over.

— JAMES BOSWELL

ened when we maximize our *customer's* position. Don't you want to buy from people who are looking out for *you*?

Everyone has a horror story to tell about taking their car to a mechanic. Many years ago, I bought a 1997 Toyota Camry off a three-year lease. I took it to my mechanic, Mike Coates, and I told him that I wanted the car to last 300,000 miles. He just smiled and said, "All right." I think he was amused at how excited I was about the car.

A few years later, I dropped my car off for Mike to go over and let me know if anything needed attention. I traveled a lot for my job and had about 170,000 miles on the car. By then, I trusted Mike. He always did good work and charged a fair price. Mike called me at my office later that morning and told me I needed a new timing belt. I asked him how much that would cost, and he told me $300. He then said that I needed two gaskets replaced. I asked him how much that would be, and he said about $300 more. I wasn't expecting that additional expense. I gasped, "Mike, do we have to fix that right now?!?" There was a pause on the other end of the phone, and I could almost see Mike smiling that big grin of his as he answered, "Yeah, if you want that car to last you 300,000 miles."

Today that car has over 400,000 miles on it because someone cared enough about *me* to remember what I told him I wanted.

It's important to realize that 80% of all the customers in the world want to work with someone who cares about them. Caring about the customer means staying on top of whatever is going on and working hard to make sure they get what they want. You help them solve their problems and treat them like a friend.

Caring is the secret ingredient in relationships. Caring is the emotional connection, the *deposit* we leave in our customers' hearts that makes them want to come back and do business with us again.

The third question is: **Can I depend on you?** Are you going to do what you promised?

If you want a strategy that will put you in front of your competitors, this is one of the best. A lot of people don't follow-through on what they say they're going to do. They may have the best of intentions but not the discipline to follow through and deliver what they promised. Your sales person says, "Listen, I promise I'll take care of you. If something goes wrong, just give me a call. Here's my cell phone number!" Then something goes wrong and you call. You get their voicemail and you leave a message. *And they don't call you back.*

Or, you tell someone you'll have what they need to them by 8:00am the next morning. You then have a really long day, it's 7:00pm at night, you haven't been home yet, and it's going to take you thirty minutes

As I grow older, I pay less attention to what men say. I just watch what they do.
— Andrew Carnegie

to put the proposal together so you can e-mail it to them and keep your promise. Are you going to do it?

If you tell someone that you are going to do something and then don't follow through and do it, you are sabotaging your success. How many times have people told you they would do something, and then didn't do it? Didn't that cause you problems, sometimes BIG problems?

So, consider the impact you have on the customers that are counting on you. If you don't follow through on your promises, they lose their faith in you and look for someone else to do business with. On the other hand, when you consistently do what you say you're going to do, customers are drawn toward you because you're one of the few that actually follow through on what you promise. That's who your customers want for a business partner. Somebody they can count on. Make it important to do whatever you tell people you're going to do, and watch your business grow.

One thing that will help you do what you promise is an organizational system, paper or electronic, where you can store your appointments, to-dos, and essential details of conversations, commitments, etc. This system needs to be capable of holding all critical information in one place for easy reference. It's extremely difficult in today's world to remember what you've promised unless you have some reliable process to help you remember every day without exception.

*People don't care
about how much you know,
until they know
how much you care.*
— CAVETT ROBERT

Question number four is: *Am I important to you?*

I once heard someone say, "I'm not much, but I'm all I ever think about." That's amusing to most of us when we really think about it, but it's also true. What's going on in our world and our life is what's most important to us and what we think about all the time.

In today's impersonal society, many of your customers are ordinary people who are starved for someone to pay a little extra attention to them and make them feel important. When we work with customers, it's time to take the spotlight we love to have pointed in our direction, and turn it around so that it's beam is full force on the customer.

The world is filled with people, your potential customers, who reward you with repeat business because you took the time to notice them and make them feel special. The faster the world turns, the more it creates people who need to have their personal worth validated by someone who takes the time to make them feel important.

One of my close friends, Dick Wilson, is a master at this. He is a highly successful business person, blessed with a beautiful and intelligent partner, Ardi. They have traveled the world and his list of friends is unbelievable. But he doesn't allow his good fortune to puff himself up. He has developed the gift of making you feel like a million bucks by focusing his conversation on what's going on in your life. When he introduces you to someone else, he always tells the other person about some accomplishment in your life or some positive aspect about who you are. You always feel a little special when you're around Dick because he makes it important to make you feel special.

Whenever he meets new people, he uses the opportunity to find out about *them*. He focuses all his attention on making them important. He constantly redirects the conversation back to them. And because he makes the person he's with feel important, they fall in love with him. People gush about how wonderful a conversationalist he is without ever realizing that he gets them to do most of the talking. He's simply a great listener and encourager.

If you'll make your customers feel important, you'll add to your customer magnetism. When you step into your work clothes, transform yourself into a listener, an encourager, and a problem solver. Put all your attention on whomever you are serving at the moment. Make it all about them, not about you. And your customers will love you for it and come back, again and again.

And the final question is: **Are you telling me the truth?** Are you giving me the information I need to know to make the best decision, or are you misrepresenting something just to get my business?

Let's face it. We all want other people to be truthful

with us. If I was aware of some really bad news that was getting ready to affect your life, would you want me to tell you as soon as possible so that you could deal with it right now, or tell you later when it might be more difficult to do something about it? I want people to tell me the good, the bad, and the ugly, so I can make realistic choices based on plain and simple facts.

In telling the truth with Customers, I'm not saying you should disclose the worst possible thing that could go wrong if they did business with you. What I'm saying is for you to have the courage and personal integrity to set realistic expectations with them, and give them honest answers to their questions. Don't tell them something you know is not true just to get their business. If a Customer says they have to have it by Friday, and you know good and well that you can't get it to them by Friday, *don't tell them you can get it to them by Friday.*

You're going to create more problems for the Customer *and* for yourself if you promise something you can't deliver. If the Customer tells you they *must* have it by Friday, tell the Customer you can't get it to them by Friday, but you *can* get it to them by the following Tuesday (if, in fact, that is true). Then ask them why Friday is so important and explore with them to see if you can discover a way to work around that. At least that approach will give you an opportunity to see if they will agree to what you *can* deliver.

You're better off walking away from a piece of business because you can't fulfill your promise than to promise what you can't deliver and have the whole thing explode in your face. When we care enough about the welfare of someone else to be honest with them, the customers with whom we want to build long-term relationships will appreciate and respect us for that. As a result, our reputation grows over time. We become a trusted partner in their business. And trusted partners are the ones who get rewarded with the most repeat business and referrals.

WHAT ARE THE CONSEQUENCES?

Are you passing the test with your customers? How would they answer these five questions about you? About your company? Why are they so important and why do they make such a difference? *Because the grades they give you determine your long-term success.*

It's just like being in school. If you do not maintain a high enough grade-point average you risk being expelled. Isn't that the way it is in life? Don't we get *expelled* from our relationships if we don't take care of them? And what does it look like when we get expelled from our relationships? Customers quit buying from us. Customers stop returning our calls. *Customers kick us out of their lives because we don't pass their test.*

Here's the *bigger* test. Are you telling yourself the truth about the grade-point average you're earning from your customers? Who does it hurt if you're not being honest about it? Your customers will put up with only so much, and then they'll move on. Who stands to gain the most from how well you score on the test?

Here's the *biggest* test. Are you willing to do what it takes to get a test score of 90% or higher with your customers every day? If you're not willing to deliver an exceptional experience to your customers every day, your business *cannot* improve its performance.

We sabotage ourselves by earning poor test scores. The formula for success is simple. If you want to have extraordinary relationships with your customers and maximize your return on investment, be trustworthy, look out for the best interest of others, do what you say you're going to do, be genuine and sincere in word and action, make them important, be honest with them, and show them how much you care about *their* success.

I've heard so many people say to me after an event, "I really enjoyed your presentation. You made some great points, and it was a good reminder of what I know I need to be doing." Listen up: It doesn't do you any good to know what you need to be doing with your customers, *if you're not doing it*. The magic happens only when you do it.

When you score an "A" on the test with your customer, you'll get:

Repeat business and referrals. You'll experience real business growth, not creative accounting growth.

Increased income and profits. If you're getting more referrals and repeat business from your customers, you're making more money.

Improved Job Satisfaction. If new business is walking in the front door and calling you on the phone, instead of you having to go out and find it, you and your employees will have more fun at work.

Strong Customer Relationships. You'll enjoy bulletproof relationships with your customers if you pass their test and give them what they want. Why? Because it's so hard for them to find a business that does that.

Trust. Cooperation. Buy-In. When you work with a Customer that trusts you, you have a lot less selling to do. They're more willing to go along with your suggestions because they trust you to make the *right* suggestions.

Guess what I do when I find businesses out there that answer these five questions successfully on a consistent basis? *I give them lots of referrals!*

Can you see the possibilities that open up when you answer these Five Questions successfully? How you can transform your business into one that attracts customers irresistibly? Earning high grades through consistently delivering Exceptional Customer Service increases your *Customer Magnetism* to attract and retain customers and grow your business.

SAVE THE CUSTOMER!

Let me share with you a BIG problem I see in the business world today. It originates from leadership not clearly explaining to every employee what their number one responsibility is. Consider this: How many of you have bought something like a washing machine or automobile, and something went wrong? You take it back to where you bought it, and you speak to someone in *service*. They say, "Oh, we can't do anything about that" or "Sorry, your warranty doesn't cover that" or just look at you like you're the biggest problem they've had all day.

The Employee doesn't understand that their *most important job* is to take a customer that walks in the front door with a problem and do whatever it takes to have them leave with a smile on their face. This is your moment of truth, when your customer has a problem. This is when they find out who you really are and if you're going to follow through on what you promised them.

When your customer has a problem, it's really a tremendous opportunity for your business *disguised* as a

problem. You're being offered the opportunity to create a *customer for life.* A customer with a problem is
like having a customer with their hair on fire. They
call you on the phone or come to see you. The first
thing to realize is that their screaming and threats are
not personal. They're not upset with you; they're upset
because they have a problem. Their hair is on fire, and
they need your help putting it out. The temptation
is to run away or hope someone else takes care of it.

But a little known secret in business is that if you have
a customer with a problem and you can help them
solve it, the odds are that they will become your customer for life. Here's what you do. You walk into
the fire with them, take them by the hand, pull them
out, and put their fire out. When you take care of
them and solve their problem, they'll love you. Wild
horses couldn't drag that Customer away from you
because you've done something for them that few
people have ever done. They never forget what you
did for them, and become one of your biggest fans.

As leaders, your responsibility is to communicate clearly with every Employee that their Number One job is
to do everything in their power to *save the Customer.*

Tell your employees, "If a Customer comes in upset,
your mission is to do whatever it takes to save the Customer, and have them leave happy. If you think the
problem is beyond the resources you have been em-

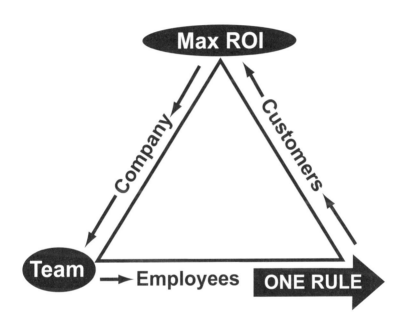

powered to use to fix it, come find me and we'll work together as a *team* to make it right for the Customer. No customer should ever leave the store without exhausting every possibility to make it right for them."

What difference does it make how well you're doing in every other function of your business, if you're not delivering an exceptional experience to your customers, then backing that up by taking care of any problems when they arise?

Customer retention and longevity, combined with sustained customer growth, is the key to higher sales, lower costs, and more profit!

Put your *primary* focus on customer retention rather than customer acquisition. Of course you want to add new customers, but it's much less expensive to hang on to the ones you already have rather than spending lots of money to attract new ones. Customer acquisition efforts should supplement customer retention, not the other way around. Get your priorities in the right order and you'll get profits in the right order.

Let's use some simple math to look at the value of customer retention. What happens when you consistently create an Exceptional Customer Experience, retain almost all of them, and get their referrals? Let's say you start out the year with 5,000 customers, and you're doing such a great job on the Customer Test that you retain 95%. That leaves you with 4,750 Customers. From the remaining 95%, you get an average of one referral per customer per year because you scored so high on their tests. The truth is, you won't get any referrals from some customers, but you'll get 3 or 4 referrals from other customers, so to keep the math simple, we'll say one referral per customer per year. That's 4,750 referrals for the year.

Now, the way a referral works is that your customer encourages a friend of theirs to do business with you, usually somebody that likes and trusts them. Your customer has said some very complimentary things about you. And with a referral, if what you offer matches what their friend is looking for, your chances of making a sale are significantly higher than if you were just out pounding on doors and making cold calls.

To keep the math as conservative and achievable as possible, let's say you convert only one out of five referrals, or 20%. Converting 20% of 4,750 referrals produces 950 new customers for the year. Add the 950 new customers to the 4,750 customers you retained during the year and you finish the year with a new total of 5,700 Customers. That's a 14% growth rate for the year, just from getting high test scores and solid referrals.

Beginning of Year:	5,000 customers
Retain 95%:	4,750 customers
ONE REFERRAL PER CUSTOMER:	4,750
Convert 20% of Referrals:	950 New Customers
End of Year:	5,700 Total Customers
Annual Growth Rate:	**14%**

How many of you enjoyed a **14% growth rate** in your Customer base last year? How much money did you spend to get those referrals? *Nothing.* Does this cause you to rethink where you invest your time and attention regarding customers? You get a whole lot more, for a whole lot less, if you make Customer retention a top priority.

Your Return on Investment improves dramatically, and employee morale goes up because it's a lot more fun working with happy customers and their referrals rather than unhappy customers. You become the overwhelming customer favorite. How much fun would *that* be?

Let's look at a great strategy about how to *retain* Customers. Let's ask the question: Why do your Customers leave you? The answer is *you don't know unless you ask them.* I've asked this question to audiences and it's a cold day in Death Valley before somebody gets correct the answer. Oh, I hear all kinds of assumptions: pricing, service, product selection, etc., but the reality is that nobody really knows unless they ask.

I was speaking at a Chamber of Commerce and someone came up to me afterwards and said, "I'm afraid to ask my customers what they think because I might not like what they say." I understand the reluctance. None of us wants to hear bad news. But wouldn't it be far better to know where you stand with your customers *today*, and what grade they're actually giving you on the test, than to watch your business slowly ride off into the sunset without knowing why? You see, it doesn't matter what kind of job *we* think we're doing; the only thing that matters is what kind of job the *customer* thinks we're doing. And the only way to find out what they think is to ask them.

In order to find out what is on the customer's mind, you need to create a *Communications Loop* with them. You want to find out what scores they're giving you on the Customer Test. Without this information, you're driving at night with your lights off in a snow storm. Your business could still be on the pavement or be sliding into a ditch. Contact your customers within two business days after they've done business with you and say: "I want to thank you again for doing business with us. I have one quick question I'd like to ask you. On a scale of 1-10, ten being that you think we hung the moon, and one meaning you're in your car right now out looking for us, what score would give us on how well we served you?"

If they give you a nine or a ten, they just gave you an "A" on the Customer Test! You say, "That's great! That's what we're shooting for! Can you give me one reason why you gave us a nine (or a ten)?" *Listen to their answer and write down exactly what they say.* Take this *Customer Feedback* and post it in public places around your company where all the Employees can see it. Point your finger at all the reasons the Customer gave you an "A" and tell everyone, "Keep doing these things! The Customers love it when we do these things!" Make sure that each team leader includes these ideas in their future plans.

If they give you a seven or an eight, you got a passing grade, but one that reflects indifference. It's not a high enough grade to ensure they'll be back. Tell them, "I really appreciate your response but I've got to tell you that's not the number we're working hard to earn from you. Can you please tell me if there is anything we can do for you *right now* that would move us to a nine or a ten? (You want to move them to a nine or ten immediately if possible). If not, can you give me one or two things we can improve so that the next time we do business together we can earn a nine or a ten?" *Listen to their answer and write down exactly what they say.* Take this *Customer Feedback* and post it with the other feedback you've received. Point

When is the best time to fix a customer problem? **RIGHT NOW!**

your finger at this feedback and say, "This is what we need to work on! The customers are telling us this is what we need to improve if we want them to keep coming back! It doesn't matter what *we* think! The only thing that matters is what the customer thinks!"

Your never-ending pursuit is to get a test score of 90% or 100% from *every* customer. An "A" (9 or 10) generates referrals and repeat business. A test score of 70% or 80% means "Yeah, you did an adequate job but I may not think about you the next time." Don't dare settle for that. A test score of 70% or 80% will not put you ahead of the competition; it will leave you in the dust of mediocrity. With mediocre profits.

If the customer gives you a six or less, *you failed their test.* Humbly communicate to them, "I sincerely apologize. We really blew it with you, and that's not acceptable. How quickly can we get together and discuss how we can fix this for you right away?" Here is where you must avoid the temptation to stick your head in the sand. You might think, "Oh, no. Now I've got to spend money out of my pocket to fix that problem."

Timeout! If you lose this customer, you're going to have to replace them with another one. Remember, it costs seven times as much to replace a customer than it does to keep an existing customer. From a purely self-serving perspective, you're better off saving an existing customer *even if it costs you something* rather than spending even more money going out in the dark and cold to find a new one. (If you don't replace them, you're slowly going out of business). By proactively taking steps to save your customers, you'll spend much less money in the long run, hang on to many more customers, and receive many more referrals. A huge payoff comes when you find a customer problem, and fix it *right away*. Feedback from customers that sing your praises about how well you're doing is always gratifying, but it's the feedback about improvements you can make or problems you can solve that will *increase your profits*.

That's why it's important to contact *all* Customers after *every* transaction because you want to find out what's going on immediately. Here's a statistic: 96% of Customers will not tell you they had a negative experience with you—they just never come back. If you get an "A" on the test, you want to let your team know immediately what the feedback was so they can focus on repeating that. And if you've delivered less than an Exceptional Customer Experience, you want to alert everyone on your team there is something that needs to be improved. NOW.

Take advantage of every opportunity to show the Customer they are important to you. Let the Customer know how much you appreciate their business, that you're not taking them for granted, and that you're willing to do whatever it takes to make it right with them, even if it costs you money. *Because they're worth it.*

Once you've polled your Customers over a period of time (a month or two based on your average number of transactions), determine your Average Test Score. Then, set a ratings goal to be achieved by a target date. You want to give your team a specific goal to shoot for. If you find your Average Test Score is a 6.9, can you set a target of 9.5 to be achieved in the next ninety days? Probably not. That's not a realistic goal.

Can you raise your Average Test Score from 6.9 to 7.5 in ninety days? That depends. It depends on how much leadership, focus, and resources you invest in your team to make the necessary changes to correct the issues that gave you the lower scores in the first place. Everyone on your team knows the goal (7.5). You've clearly explained what issues have been identified by the Customer Feedback, so everyone understands what must be improved to raise the score. Everyone on your team works together, with you leading the way, to make the necessary adjustments and hit the target. Then, when they've achieved an average customer rating of 7.5, you *celebrate* your *team's* success and raise the bar again.

You may be thinking, "Why do I want to call up every Customer and find out what they think? My goodness, that seems like a lot of work. I don't have time to do that. I can't devote the resources to make that happen. We're busy all the time . . ." Yammer, yammer, yammer. A better question to ask is when are you going to have the time and money to go out in the jungle and find new Customers to replace the ones that are disappearing?

When you connect with your Customers, when you ask them for their feedback on how well you're serving their needs, it communicates something very powerful to them. It gives them the attention they crave, makes them feel important, and provides them the opportunity to tell you what they *think* and what they *want* from doing business with you. They'll tell you how to hang on to them if you'll ask them. Then, make sure you follow through on what they say!

Here's why this is such an incredible opportunity: *Nobody else is doing that for your customers in the marketplace.* Nobody out there is showing they care enough about their Customers to call them up and ask them, "We really appreciate your business! What do you think? How well are we doing? What can we do to improve it?" When you use this powerful and effective strategy to connect with your Customers, it strengthens their loyalty and gives them one more reason to refer you. And, it gives you the EXACT information you need every single day to get more business, earn more profits, achieve more growth, and enjoy more success. Who *wouldn't* want to do that?

Are you looking for a *Great Idea*, an opportunity of enormous potential, to get your Customer's attention and keep them around for a long time? Then re-read the last section and make it happen. No procrastination, no excuses. And make sure you've got plenty of enthusiastic Employees to handle the steady increase in business.

THE LEADERSHIP PRIORITY

The Wind and the Sun were arguing which was the stronger. Suddenly they saw a traveler coming down the road, and the Sun said: "I see a way to decide our dispute. Whichever of us can cause that traveler to take off his cloak shall be regarded as the stronger. You begin." So the Sun retired behind a cloud, and the Wind began to blow as hard as it could upon the traveler. But the harder he blew the more closely did the traveler wrap his cloak round him, till at last the Wind had to give up in despair. Then the Sun came out and shone in all his glory upon the traveler, who soon found it too hot to walk with his cloak on.

AESOP'S FABLES

A lot of leaders think they want as much power over as many people, places, and things as possible. The truth is, trust, encouragement, and empowerment will serve you far better than power. You'll get more of the results you want through persuasion and encouragement than by intimidation or force.

What is the biggest contribution a leader can make to their organization to maximize its success? A leader's most effective tool is *building morale*. A leader builds morale through inspiration, encouragement, and providing the quality of support that helps *everybody else* in the organization be successful. Morale is the electrical current running through the organization that keeps everybody energized. Daniel Goleman wrote in his landmark book, <u>Emotional Intelligence</u>, that "A two percent rise in attitude equals a one per cent rise in productivity."[1] If you can increase the morale and the attitudes of your Employees, then enthusiasm, productivity *and* profits will go up. *You'll get more of everything you want* by increasing the attitudes and morale of your Employees.

Autocratic, top-down leadership doesn't maximize the potential of today's Employees. A paradigm shift is needed in the way leadership views their role in order to maximize productivity and sustain positive attitudes. The type of relationship with your employees that will help you get everything you want can be found in the type of relationship you want to enjoy with your customers.

---

[1] Goleman, Daniel. 2005. *Emotional Intelligence*. New York: Bantam Books.

If you want to have Customers respond enthusiastically to what you offer, you must offer them what they want. The closer you can make your offer match what they want, the more Customers and business you'll enjoy.

The same is true of your Employees. In order to activate and energize their full potential, you must help them get what they want from work.

In order of importance, Employees want:

The Top Ten Things your employees want are:

1. Purpose

2. Goals

3. Responsibilities

4. Autonomy

5. Flexibility

6. Attention

7. Opportunities for innovation

8. Open-mindedness

9. Transparency

10. Compensation[2]

---

[2]Lapowsky, Issie. "Inc.." 08/27/2010.http://www.inc.com/guides/2010/08/10-things-employees-want.html (accessed 10/17/2010).

Compensation—paychecks, vacations, health insurance—
is only one item on their list. The other nine "wants" have
nothing to do with money, and everything to do with being
respected, valued, and provided with an active role in the
company. If you want to attract and retain the best employees out there, you'll need to create a work environment that
provides what today's employees want. If you won't make
these changes, you'll continue to fight turnover and morale
issues, which result in higher costs and lower productivity.

Here are a few ideas on increasing morale and attitudes:

Help your Employees get what they want. Take an active role in discovering what your direct reports want out
of their jobs. Discover their internal motivators. Ask
them about their "why": why are they working, what are
their goals and dreams, what motivates them, and how
they prefer to be rewarded beyond the paycheck. Then,
together, help them think through the process and come
up with a personal plan for them to get what they want.

Eliminate Obstacles. As a Leader, eliminating obstacles that are in your Employees' way—due to dysfunctional work processes, breakdown of communications,
office/work group politics, departments that won't work
together, or whatever—is *your* responsibility. Don't assume that the conflicting parties will find a successful
resolution by either fighting it out or being ignored by
you. They won't. The ostrich strategy is a coward's
strategy, not the strategy of a leader. When your em-

ployees see you abandoning the helm when they need you most, they lose hope and sink to the level of doing just enough to get by. If you don't care enough to support *them* 100% by using your authority to eliminate the obstacles that get in their way, then, right or wrong, you strip them of the motivation to give *you* 100%.

The best manager I ever worked for, Jay Jackson, was someone I could take my obstacles to and he'd say, "I'll take care of that for you. I'll make that go away. Go back to selling something." And it was a wonderful feeling as an Employee to be able to take those problems to him and get them off my back so I could focus on the job I was paid to do. I knew that Jay would make those things go away. I didn't have to worry about them anymore. I couldn't make those problems go away because I didn't have the authority and it wasn't in my job description. But as a manager and leader, *he could and he did.*

Encourage your Employees to be their best. Encourage them to learn every day from what they're doing, especially from their mistakes. I heard a story about an IBM employee who made a decision that cost the company millions. He was called to his boss' office, certain he was about to be fired. When he asked about that, his boss roared, "Do you think I'm going to fire you after all that money I just paid for your education?"

Leadership is about helping those you're responsible for grow and succeed. Focus on the positive, or at

Focus on growing the quality of your people and the morale of your team, not the quantity of output. The output will take care of itself.

— JEFF PEDEN

least the lesson that can be learned from the mistake. Hold onto the big picture of what you want the Employee to eventually achieve, but help them get there one small step at a time. Discuss with your Employee what is working and how to incrementally improve on it. Make it a positive environment for them to grow and thrive in, instead of focusing on the negative and stopping enthusiasm in its tracks. Be their biggest cheerleader, because every time they win, you win.

Provide ongoing learning opportunities. Encourage and support the members of your team that want to improve and grow. The people that step forward today to advance themselves are your future leaders. They're demonstrating enthusiasm, initiative, and development potential. They're motivated, ambitious and willing to put in extra effort to succeed. They're the ones you *want* leading teams in your organization. Provide them the resources to accomplish their goals: internal and external learning opportunities, continuing education/technical training, college degrees and graduate courses related to their work. Be willing to spend the time to mentor them as much as they want. Support their growth and they will repay you with enthusiasm, productivity, and undying loyalty.

If you are offering internal learning opportunities, then train your team with the best. Don't assume that information is just information, and it doesn't matter who delivers it. Find the best person you can afford to teach your people how to improve their performance. Don't expect the Human Resource department to deliver all of the knowledge and skills development your organization needs. That's an impossible and unfair assignment. They're great at what they've been trained to do, but to hold them accountable for teaching your people effective skills in areas beyond their own personal experience is unfair to them and those who need to advance their skills.

For example, if you want to improve your team's ability to develop new business, and no one in HR has any significant business development experience, find someone to do the job with a proven track record of success and whose philosophy matches your corporate values. This person could be someone that already works for you and would love the opportunity to share their wealth of knowledge with fellow team members. Your employees and your company deserve the best resources you can find for them, inside or outside the company. If it's a skill that truly needs developing, find someone that excels at that skill and pay them what they're worth to do the job. It will create the results you want faster and cost you less in the long run.

Lead with Influence. I believe the most effective leadership structure today functions from the bottom up, not the top down. In this model, the CEO's responsibility is to support the success of *everyone* in

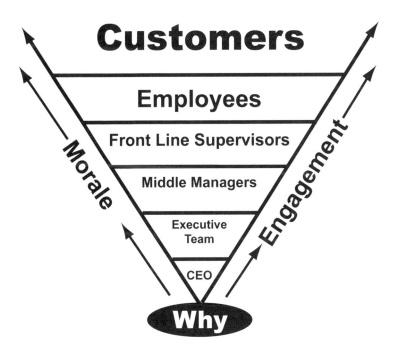

the organization, and to eliminate any obstacles that may hinder those efforts. One of the CEO's primary responsibilities is to anticipate future needs and opportunities for their Company, and to provide the necessary resources to grow and be ready for the future.

Effective leadership uses their wisdom and experience to influence and engage everybody in their organization. At every level, leaders are responsible and accountable to work with their direct reports to help them be as successful as possible. Your success as a Leader is ultimately defined by the success or failure of your team. General Colin Powell once said what he had to learn about being an effective leader was that it was not about him; it was all about his troops. It was only when *they* were successful that he achieved success as a leader.

Ultimately, everyone in leadership is responsible to throw their support behind the front-line employees, because they are the team members that make direct contact with the customer. Why is that so critical to the success of everyone else in the company? *Because the customer is the only reason for your existence as a business.* If front-line employees are supported in every way to deliver an Exceptional Experience for the Customer, the customer will reward the entire company with repeat business and referrals, profits and growth.

Create a compelling purpose for your organization's existence. It is the responsibility of leadership to provide the *Why*. Victor Frankl, a Viennese psychiatrist who survived the concentration camps of World War II, learned through his experiences that if someone can create a big enough *Why*, the *How* will take care of itself. Why are you in the business you're in? What benefits are you providing your customers? Is it something you can be proud of? Does it serve your customers in a way that fills their needs and supports their happiness? Does it give meaning and purpose to your own life? Is it a big enough *Why* to make it worth all the time you invest? Is it big enough for your employees to get excited about and put their hearts into?

Create a Why that's big enough, bold enough, and morally strong enough to inspire the best from your team. Share that Why with every level of your Company, and reinforce it by the behaviors and attitudes your leaders model every day.

Take responsibility. Finally, a Leader must take responsibility for the outcomes their team creates. One of my favorite characters in American history is Harry Truman. On Harry's desk in the Oval Office was a little plaque that said, "The Buck Stops Here." Harry, an old Army artillery officer in World War I, was familiar with the practice of passing the buck. But, Harry was wise enough to realize there wasn't anyone higher in command in the United States to pass the buck to beyond himself. Ultimately, he knew he had to take responsibility for all the positive *and* negative outcomes resulting from the decisions he made.

A true leader takes responsibility for all outcomes. It is only through taking responsibility for everything that a leader empowers themselves to make changes in the recipe in order to change the outcomes of future decisions.

DEVELOP A GREAT COMPANY

One of the greatest opportunities leaders have today to outperform their competition is to create a work environment where Employees can thrive. How can leadership do that?

- Do a great job hiring people that are customer-centric. Don't hire bodies to fill gaps; hire people that have people skills and a personality that fits the job. Add people to your team that fit in well with your culture. Be careful who you add to your mix; they must be capable of buying into your strategic mission, company values, and what you are working to accomplish.

- Take extraordinary care of the people you hire. Regardless of your business model, make sure your company does everything it can to make it a fun, growth-centered, and family-oriented place to work. Make your employees feel welcomed, appreciated, and cared for every day. That means you need to make sure you have a management team in

place that has strong people skills and enjoys looking out for and developing the talent and potential
of others.

- Make it important to offer your employees a future,
  not just a job. Give them a place to work where
  they can get benefits and enough hours to pay their
  bills, live their life, and grow professionally. If you
  hire a bunch of part-time workers to avoid paying
  benefits, that's exactly what you'll get: a bunch of
  part-time employees that don't care about you any
  more than you care about them. You'll have to
  keep replacing them over and over at a cost that
  far exceeds good, full time employees with benefits.
  Hire the right people and give them a great place
  to work where they have every reason to help you
  achieve your goals.

- Invest in teaching your people the skills to perform their jobs successfully. This means having
  a management team that is personally involved
  in encouraging and developing every person on
  their team. Most companies have something at
  the beginning of employment where such things
  as policies and procedures are explained. This is
  not enough to create a workforce that is going to
  produce extraordinary results. You must provide
  them the ongoing education and support necessary
  to maximize their potential and shape them into
  productive and contributing team members.

- Create a work environment where the culture is based on looking out for others and doing the right thing. You'll attract and retain better employees while generating stronger profits and better growth. You'll also create a work environment that provides important meaning to everyone's work.

- Develop a management team that embodies and models the character traits your customers and employees want most. Can your leadership team be trusted? Do they care about the best interest of your customers and employees? Do they follow-through on what they promise? Do they make their team feel like they're an important part of the organization and ask for their opinions and ideas? Are they known for telling the truth? You can't succeed with your employees and your customers unless your leaders lead the way in *every* way.

THE VELOCITY OF IDEAS

There's a concept in Economics called the *Velocity of Money*. It means that money travels through our economy at a certain speed which reflects how well the overall economy is doing. When money travels slowly from person to person and from business to business, the economy is doing poorly. What happens when times are bad? People *hang on* to their money. As the Velocity of Money increases, the health and vibrancy of the economy improves as well.

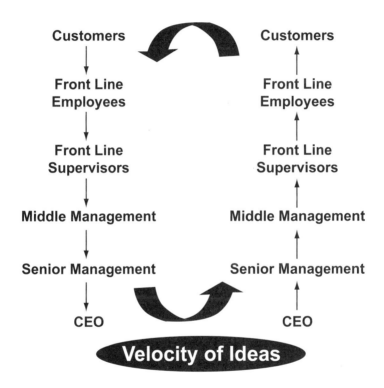

The same is true about **The Velocity of Ideas.** The fewer ideas a Company has about improving morale and productivity, solving problems, increasing sales, improving customer satisfaction, lowering costs, etc, the slower the company makes progress. On the other hand, if a Company can access a continuous flow of ideas on how to improve what they're doing, they increase their ability to make corrections and improve their performance.

In order to accelerate the Velocity of Ideas, you must be willing to include your Employees as full team members. They must understand how important they are to the performance and success of your business. You must ask for their ideas and empower them as *Problem Solvers*, then reward them for their contributions.

Of equal value is communicating with your Customers daily. Ask them to share their experience of you—what they like, don't like, and their suggestions for improvement—and gather valuable observations from their perspective.

When consistently encouraged and rewarded, ideas generated by your Employees and your Customers will gain in velocity. Leadership begins to receive an incredible flow of useful information about how to improve performance and create more effective and longer lasting results. You no longer have to figure out everything by yourself! Your employees and customers will do that for you if you'll just *ask them*. They will create a Velocity of Valuable Ideas you can use to make the best decisions, move your business ahead of the competition, and *keep it there*.

Let's conclude: In order for a company to maximize their return on investment, the first thing a company has to do is create a TEAM with their Employees that forms one complete picture, where all the parts are connected together in the right order. Everybody on the team can count on the support and assistance of everyone else. There's no "me" versus "them". As a result, morale, productivity and cooperation are high. This TEAM has the ability to deliver what the customer wants and earn an "A" on their test.

Then, the TEAM filters all decisions and actions through the One Rule: *Always do what's in the best interest of the Customer.* The TEAM works together to deliver an Exceptional Customer Experience that creates repeat business and referrals and drives profits and growth. Work becomes a place Employees want to be a part of because they're all involved in a game that's fun to play. The game is called, "How can we work together today and get A's on our customer tests?" It's amazing how clearly defined targets achieve clearly intended results.

The customers are included by being asked for their feedback and suggestions for improvement. They feel appreciated and listened to because no one else cares enough to ask. They reward you with their loyalty and support.

When you implement the strategies outlined in this book, you will receive the following benefits:

- *Profits and business growth.* What do you think you'd achieve if you raised morale and increased productivity while getting a constant stream of new ideas on how to run your business better? Not to mention all the referrals from customers in love with you? How could you NOT make more money? It's a no-brainer.

- *Teamwork, commitment, and engagement.* People like working for an organization that looks out for them. If you empower their active participation toward accomplishing clearly defined targets, their morale and productivity will go sky high! Employees will change from being indifferent to their jobs and performing at a fraction of their potential, to looking forward to being a important and useful member of a team, every day.

- *Attract higher-quality employees.* The more supportive you are toward your employees, helping them get what they want from work, and creating a fun work environment, the better the Employee you will attract over time. People today want to work where they are wanted, valued, and respected.

- *Better decision-making based on The One Rule.* If you will ask the question, "What effect will this have on the customer?" before making decisions

and taking action, you'll create more profitable results. The *One Rule* is your guiding light that keeps
your company on the path of growth while protect-
ing it from outside threats. If it costs seven times
as much to attract a new customer as it does to
keep an existing customer, why *wouldn't* you want
to always do the best thing for them to keep them
happy and coming back? Don't allow yourself to
get focused on short-term results at the expense of
long-term success.

* **Reduces stress significantly while increasing your
enjoyment of work.** If you developed a team that
supported each other's success, systematically elim-
inated all barriers to productivity and communication, and sustained an open exchange of ideas on
how to achieve goals, then a lot more work would
get done in a lot less time. A highly effective and
interdependent work environment eliminates a
significant amount of stress for both your employees *and* management team. How much would that
contribute to the mental and emotional health of
their lives, their marriages, their families, and their
communities? *All the difference in the world.*

What better way can you imagine to Take It
to the Max?

Some things you miss because they're so tiny you overlook them. But some things you don't see because they're so huge.
— ROBERT PIRSIG,
ZEN AND THE ART OF MOTORCYCLE MAINTENANCE

A Vision for the Future

From time to time an idea comes along that can improve your organization's effectiveness. But every once in a while a *Great Idea* comes along that can change the entire landscape of your battlefield. *This is it.* If you will transform your organization into one that focuses on doing what's in the best interest of your employees and customers and insist on delivering an Exceptional Customer Experience *every time*, you will blow away the competition *and* get everything you want in terms of dollars and cents. And, you will live a life where you feel good about who you are and what you do for a living.

The most important action you can take for the health and profitability of your business is to begin putting these ideas into practice today. Nothing has greater power to leverage your return on investment. With all the potential benefits on the table, isn't it worth giving these ideas a fair chance in your organization? Maybe you can't implement them simultaneously in every division of your company. But start somewhere *today*. Let the results speak for themselves. Once you begin to achieve results from the application of these ideas, you won't need any more outside encouragement. You'll get all the enthusiasm and incentive you need from inside your own organization. And, you'll be on your way to being a part of an organization that you've always dreamed of.

Our Mission

Our Time
Our Money

Our Culture
Our People Processes

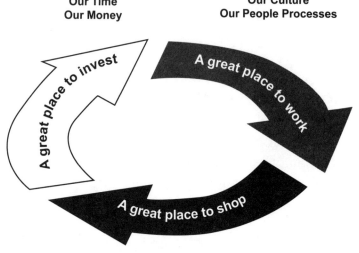

A great place to invest

A great place to work

A great place to shop

Our People
Our Customers
Our Stores
Our Coffee
Our Subs

REAL-LIFE APPLICATIONS

QUICK CHEK, NEWARK, NJ

Here is an inside view into the successful application of some major ideas in the book. I was invited to visit Quick Chek's Corporate Offices and Support Center on August 18-19, 2010 to compare notes and observe their business model.

Quick Chek is headquartered in Whitehouse Station, NJ. Established in 1967 by Carlton C. Durling, who owned a dairy farm and wanted to take advantage of the emerging convenience store industry for dairy product sales, Quick Chek has grown to 125 stores located throughout New Jersey and New York, with 2,600 employees.

The first thing I noticed was the enthusiasm, excitement, and positive attitudes of everyone I met. Walking down a corporate corridor and having people give me a friendly greeting without knowing who I was or what I was doing there was refreshing. It appeared that everyone enjoyed their work and was committed to creating "A Great Place to Work" (more on that later). They walked the talk every day, beginning with the President and CEO.

In discussions with Dean Durling, CEO and President, Mike Murphy, Senior Vice President of Operations, Bob Graczyk, Vice President of Human Resources, and John Schaninger, Vice President of Sales & Marketing, they were of one accord about what it takes to drive an organization toward excellence. All shared three major themes they pursued daily: Always do the right thing (for both employees and customers), maintain a "restless dissatisfaction" toward current levels of achievement, and ask constantly in every situation: **Would this make Quick Chek a Great Place To Work?**

In conversations with Dean, he noted that one of the problems many organizations face today is that they focus on creating a great place to shop before first establishing a great place to work. He remarked that the model Wall Street relies on so heavily—stockholder return in the short-run—is not a sustainable model. Rather, the correct sequence to focus on and follow that sustains profits and growth is:

Create a Great Place To Work, then

Create a Great Place To Shop, which will result in

A Great Place To Invest

A substantial part of that "investment" is in the form of a profit sharing program that distributes approximately 30% of annual profits back to their own employees. This is a performance incentive that everyone in the company buys into. A substantial portion of remaining profits is invested back in the company every year: new store development, and existing store remodeling, that results in a growing organization, providing a solid future for its employees and continual opportunities for career advancement.

As a result of their focus on their mission, they have achieved the following:

- 33% of industry average in employee turnover

- Four times industry average sales volume per store

- 100% internal promotions

- Highest customer ratings

- Named "Best Places to Work in New Jersey 2010"

There are a number of axioms that Quick Chek uses to keep them focused on their core values and moving forward in accomplishing their goals. I have included a few that I picked up from my visit with them. I'm sure they are not inclusive, yet represent those I heard repeatedly from not only leaders, but from employees working on the line in several stores we visited.

They are (in no particular order):

- If we can accomplish our Mission by successfully living our Core Values and Behaviors, we can drive A Great Place To Work. The question we ask ourselves every day is: Do our actions and decisions result in A Great Place To Work?

- Insist on Standards, Excellence, and Consistency.

- Focus on People: The learning curve of the application of Core Values and Behaviors takes time.

- Create Great Leaders and put them in leadership positions. Have the right leader in place and you'll attract Great Employees—this leads to Great Customer Service.

- Always do the right thing for the customer. Even if that means apologizing for their inconvenience, refunding their money, replacing their product at no charge, and giving them a complementary cup of coffee or fountain drink for their trouble—all at no charge. They're worth too much to us to have them leave the store less than completely satisfied.

- Provide open channels of communication from Day One. Set the example and give them permission to communicate with anyone in the organization. Have an "Open Door" policy and provide cell phone numbers of top leadership to everyone in the organization.

- Catch your people doing it right. If there is a problem, determine the root cause. What it due to an employee issue or a customer issue? Ask the question: How can we prevent it from happening again?

- Never think that we know it all.

- Have the guts and discipline to change. Then, execute that change consistently every day.

And, there are some critical ideas and challenges issued to leadership:

- What are you modeling? What do you accept? Create the environment you want that produces the results you want.

- Everything starts with you. Have you asked yourself why you're not getting the results you want?

- The buck STARTS here!

As you will note in the following material, excerpted from company materials, Mission Statements, Core Values and Behaviors, and leadership and employee training materials, they use clear targets and well-defined expectations that every employee is held accountable to know and successfully execute. This is what separates them from the competition, drives sustainable growth and profits, and forges an all-for-one and one-for-all work environment that is at the same time internally contagious and externally attractive to their customers and future team members (most of their new hires come from internal referrals and store signage).

Voted one of the best places to work in New Jersey in 2010 by their own employees, **they put into practice every day** the values, behaviors and beliefs that drive them to excellence. As they have consistently done so for the last fifteen years, and as they continue to hold themselves personally accountable for their future, Quick Chek is indeed a Great Place To Work, A Great Place To Shop, and A Great Place To Invest!

OUR MISSION:
A GREAT PLACE TO WORK, A GREAT PLACE TO SHOP, AND A GREAT PLACE TO INVEST

CORE VALUES AND BEHAVIORS

Strong Leadership
- Demonstrates integrity and honesty (does the right thing).
- Holds self accountable for team's personal growth and success.
- Communicates clear goals and expectations to others through regular team meetings.
- Empowers others to think and take action.
- Recognizes others for their achievements.

Total Customer Dedication
- Actively listens to understand the needs and emotions of our customers.
- Uses customer and team feedback to exceed expectations.
- Anticipates the customers' needs and expectations.
- Provides a great customer experience.
- Strives to maintain quality and cleanliness standards.

Act Like the Owner
- Sets and achieves goals to get the right results.
- Pays attention to the details.
- Acts with a sense of urgency.
- Takes responsibility and will not pass it on.

Be the Best You Can Be
- Is committed to continuous learning for self.
- Demonstrates a positive attitude every day.
- Embraces change and encourages new ideas.
- Values a balance between personal and professional life.
- Shows a sense of humor—has fun at work.

"Play to Win"
- Solves problems and addresses the cause.
- Seeks and gives open and honest feedback.
- Actively participates in all huddles and meetings.
- Is committed to achieving the team's goals.
- Is willing to take risks to get results.

Caring
- Actively supports Quick Chek as a partner in the community.
- Listens to our neighbors and reacts to their issues and concerns.
- Maintains caring relationships with team members and customers.
- Maintains a safe place for team members and customers.

Dear New Team Member,

Welcome to Quick Chek!

By now, you may have heard of or seen our mission, A Great Place To Work, A Great Place To Shop and A Great Place To Invest". While the words may seem somewhat different to you, the message is essentially the same: **Total Customer Dedication.**

In order to achieve Total Customer Dedication (TCD), however, you must first make Quick Chek "A Great Place To Work". If you have fun and enjoy yourself and each other, our customers will also have a fun and satisfying experience at our stores. Everybody wins! I'm very proud to tell you our team members voted us one of New Jersey's "Best Places To Work" in 2010.

To support our goal of Total Customer Dedication, we live by core values. You will notice that the number one core value is Strong Leadership. Strong Leaders build strong teams by encouraging communication, personal development, and, of course, fun.

You will see many examples of leaders, leaders-in-the-making and people striving to "Be The Best They Can Be" (Core Value #2). And how about "Playing To Win" (Core Value #3)? If that phrase isn't familiar yet, it will be soon.

When you "Play To Win", you commit to going all-out in your personal and professional endeavors instead of playing it safe. I'm here to tell you that "Playing To Win" is satisfying and exhilarating beyond belief! Here at Quick Chek you will be trained and learn that "Playing To Win" becomes a way of doing things. I hope to meet you in your store real soon. Again, welcome to Quick Chek!

Dean Durling
President and CEO

(Excerpted from the Quick Chek Team Member Handbook)

NEW TEAM MEMBER INFORMATION

"The Quick Chek Experience"

The Quick Chek Experience is the foundation for everything we do. As a new team member you will learn the policies and Quick Chek practices that make Quick Chek a Great Place To Work. You will learn that our customers are the reason we exist and our attitude towards them ensures a Great Place To Shop for all our customers. New team members must attend The Quick Chek Experience before serving customers.

1. The customer is **ALWAYS RIGHT.**

2. On our company organization chart, our customer is at the top and the President and Vice Presidents are at the bottom.

3. The customer is our most important asset.

4. Also as important an asset to our company is our store team. **THE TEAM IS QUICK CHEK.**

5. Each member of a store team is responsible for TCD "The Experience". Your attitude is key to your store's success.

6. Each member of the store team will be correctly trained in our customer experience standards.

7. Each store leader will ensure that our store team works together so that the store is continuously customer friendly and customer focused.

8. Everything we do that could possibly affect our customer must be communicated in a positive way.

9. We are a convenience retail food store with gas and

pharmacy services available at many locations. Therefore, The Customer Experience is a Safe, Clean store; Fresh products and Friendly, Efficient service.

10. All of these are accomplished by you, our team member. It's your attitude and belief that servicing and selling to people is rewarding an fun to do.

11. All new team members will be scheduled to attend the TCD "The Experience" class at the Support Center or other company training sites on their first day of employment.

(Excerpted from the Quick Chek Team Member Handbook)

BE OUR G.U.E.S.T.!

GREET:
- Greet each and every customer
- Make sure you mean it
- Make it friendly and natural so customers feel welcome; remember you are the host!
- Get your customer to feel "WOW" because of your service.

UNDERSTAND:
- Understand what your customers need
- Talk to them!
- Imagine your customers are guests coming to your home
- Take note of your customers' moods

EYE CONTACT:
- Look your customers in the eye
- Show that you are paying attention
- "Be There" for your customers

SPEEDY SERVICE:
- Good customer service depends on speed
- Keep your cool; size up with your customer needs and take care of them
- Reassure customers that you will be right with them

THANK:
- Make a good last impression
- After taking care of your customer, be sure to say, "Thank you". It sounds obvious, but sometimes we forget. And don't forget to ask them to come back!

(Excerpted from "The Quick Chek Experience" Participant's Workbook)

CUSTOMER RECOVERY:
MAKING A L.A.S.T.ing IMPRESSION

Listen
- Listen to the customer immediately; stop whatever you are doing!
- Face the customer and look into their eyes
- Allow the customer to tell their story
- Empathize and ask questions to understand; this will show that you are acknowledging that they are upset
- Don't get sidetracked by distractions; "be there" with the customer

Apologize
- Apologize without condition and with no hint of defensiveness or shifting blame (watch your body language—crossed arms, rolling eyes, and sighing will tell the customer you are not sincere)

- Deliver an apology in the first person—"I" statements are so much more meaningful. ("I am sorry for..." or "I apologize for..." is the most powerful form of an apology). The corporate "we're sorry" lacks authenticity and sincerity.

Solve

- Solve the problem quickly and fairly. Make the customer say "WOW"!

- After you acknowledge the emotions the customer is feeling, correct the customer's problems as soon as possible. Ask the customer what they would like. Generally, customers who purchase the wrong product want it exchanged for the right product, so exchange it... no questions asked.

- Generally, customers who purchase a spoiled or out-of-date product want it exchanged for a fresh product... so exchange it... no questions asked. Since we inconvenienced them, give them a refund and fresh product.

- Customers who ask if you have a certain product and you are out-of-stock are not going to be pleased. Apologize, offer an alternative product and inform them when the product requested will be back in stock. Give the customer a "Raincheck Discount Card" to use at their next visit. Ask the customer for their name and number and call them when the product comes in.

Thank

- Say "THANK YOU" to a customer. Tell the customer you appreciate their comments. Remember, a customer comment is a gift. It gives us an opportunity to make it right!

(Excerpted from "The Quick Chek Experience" Participant's Workbook)

General Improvement Ideas

- It all starts with YOU: your mindset, your skill sets and the tool sets you choose to use. Be open to feedback and to changing the way you lead your store.

- For each Driver (internal metric/goal) that you want to improve, ask yourself the following questions:
    - To what extent do I contribute to this score?
    - What can I start doing to improve this score?
    - What can I stop doing to improve this score?
    - What can I continue to do to improve this score?

- Be a great role model. If there is a change you want to see in your team or score, demonstrate that change in your own behavior first.

- Make improvement important. Talk about it in every meeting and every conversation.

- Ask for support from other Store Leaders, your District Leader, and your Team Members. Remember: "I have to do it myself, and I can't do it alone."

- When you see improvement in yourself or others, acknowledge and celebrate! Positive reinforcement leads to permanent behavior change.

STORE DRIVERS

Customer Orientation

Definition: A total team focus on the customer, understanding and delivering what our customers want, and providing a great customer experience every day.

What It Looks Like:
- We are patient and helpful with customers.
- We act on customer feedback.
- We treat each customer as an individual.
- We have clear authority to solve customer problems.
- We emphasize customer service over inventory control.

How To Improve:
- Do you view customer comments and complaints as feedback; not positive or negative, but simply information to use to improve your service?
- Do you put the customer first ALWAYS?
- Do you role model customer orientation for your team?
    - Do you take care of Team Members so they can take care of customers?

TEAMWORK

Definition: Working together to provide a great experience for our customers through open and honest communication among all Team Members.

What It Looks Like:
- We operate as a team, not as individuals.
- We rely on one another for support and development.
- We talk openly and honestly with each other.

- We all enjoy coming to work.

- We work together to reduce frustrations and problems.

- We address and resolve conflicts among Team Members.

How To Improve:

- Do you model the Core Values? (See Core Values)

- Does your team model Core Values?

- Do you communicate openly and honestly with your team?

- Do you encourage all Team Members to communicate openly and honestly?

- Do you hold yourself accountable for the success of your team?

- Do you encourage Team Members to hold themselves accountable or the success of **your team?**

DEVELOPMENT

Definition: We want all Team Members to be the best they can be, and provide support and opportunities for personal development.

What It Looks Like:
- We get training that helps us do our jobs better.

- We get Performance Appraisals that help us improve our performance.

- We emphasize proper training for all Team Members.

How To Improve:
- Create an environment that encourages Development

- Empower Team Members to take risks, make decisions and learn from mistakes.

- Discuss development with every Team Member every day through conversations and meetings.

- Have a written Development Plan in place for each Team Member.

- Discuss training expectations with each Team Member and make sure Team Members are trained before they are expected to do a job.

- Ensure that Team Members are scheduled for and attend required training.

- Promote often.

- Demonstrate and coach integrity by delivering on your promises.

MANAGER DRIVERS

Manages People

Definition: As a leader, I provide leadership and coaching that allows Team Members to provide a great customer experience and grow in their jobs.

What It Looks Like:
- I help Team Members develop the skills and abilities they need.

- I recognize when Team Members have done a good job.

- I allow Team Members to make decisions whenever possible.

- I carefully listen to and consider the concerns of Team Members.

- I am open and honest with Team Members.

- I communicate the reasons for decisions made that affect the work of Team Members.

- I give Team Members timely feedback about their work performance.

- I keep Team Members informed about things they need to know.

- I discuss the Strategic Plan with Team Members, and clarify how Team Members' activities are connected to our Mission, Strategy and Values.

How To Improve:
- Prepare your Team Members to do their best.

- Understand the training and development needs of all Team Members.

- Train all New Hires thoroughly before they work alone.

- Ensure every Team Member has "Ownership".

- Support your Team Members to do their best.

- Talk to Team Members every day.

- Empower Team Members to take risks, make decisions and learn from mistakes.

- Ensure Team Members comply or communicate (a process that provides the forum for discussion).

- Be direct and honest in all conversations.

- Have the difficult conversations when necessary to address performance issues.

- Review the Strategic Plan for the company and discuss how the Team's activities contribute to the company goals.

Manages Customers

Definition: As a leader, I provide a great customer experience every day.

What It Looks Like:
- I am skilled at handling customers.
- I demonstrate my belief that serving customers is the first priority.
- I create an environment that motivates people.
- I take a positive rather than a negative approach to things.

How To Improve:
- Ask customers "What could we do better?"
- Create energy and include the customers in the fun.
- Be a role model for a fun and inviting environment, and encourage Assistant Store Leaders and Shift Leaders to role model as well.
- Empower Team Members to solve customer issues with no questions asked.
- Coach Team Members to put customers first, tasks second.

Empowerment

Definition: As a leader, I provide Team Members with the freedom, coaching and support to make decisions that provide a great customer experience.

What It Looks Like:

- Team Members are clear about the decisions they can make on their own without asking anyone.

- Team Members are able to make decisions without too many approvals and steps

- The information Team Members need to make decisions is available.

How To Improve:

- Give "ownership" of each shift to the Team Members on that shift.

- Coach Team Members to resolve problems on their own.

Role Of The Store Leader

You have three major roles as a Store Leader:

1. **Creator of Culture**

   Culture is defined as "the formally or informally agreed upon beliefs and behaviors that are accepted in an organization." In other words, "the way things are around here."

   Culture is created by people, not companies. It is how we "show up" each day, the quantity and quality of conversations we have and the values we live. As a Store Leader, you have the key role in creating and maintaining your store's culture. You can't just talk about culture; you have to live it.

2. **Leader**

A leader is someone that people follow because they want to, not because they have to.

A Manager's job is to keep things the way they are. A Leader's job is to create change. Both are important; you may manage when you want to maintain standards. But to improve standards, you have to lead.

3. **Coach**

Great Coaches:

- Are patient, caring and understanding when developing Team Members.

- Take time to:

  i. Explain what to do, how to do it and why it is done that way.

  ii. Demonstrate the proper way to do it.

  iii. Have Team Members practice the new behavior.

- Compliment and recommend alternatives.

- Provide encouragement, support and positive reinforcement.

- Challenge Team Members to do their best.

- Encourage Team Members to enjoy their work.

(Excerpted from the Quick Chek TCD Leadership Toolkit)